Montréal

A guide to recent architecture

•••

Steven Ware

Montréal

A guide to recent architecture

• • • ellipsis

•••

BRITISH LIBRARY CATALOGUING IN PUBLICATION
A CIP record for this book is available from the British Library

PUBLISHED BY •••ellipsis
2 Rufus Street London N1 6PE
E MAIL ...@ellipsis.co.uk
WWW http://www.ellipsis.com
EDITOR Annie Bridges
SERIES EDITOR Tom Neville

ISBN 1 8899858 60 1

PRINTING AND BINDING Hong Kong

For a copy of the Ellipsis catalogue or information on special quantity orders of Ellipsis books please contact us on 020 7739 3157 or sales@ellipsis.co.uk

Montréal: a guide to recent architecture

Steven Ware 2001

Contents

Introduction

The projects described in this book date back to 1983. There are 100 in all, forming a selection which I hope will represent the broadest possible range of architectural production. Being neither resident nor native of Montréal, I have allowed the text to become anthropological in its outlook, treating the architectural project as a cultural artefact which is inextricably associated with the people it serves. In researching the guide I visited the buildings, read reports in both the architectural and general press, and spoke to members of the architectural profession and public alike. The texts and conversations which accompany the projects are intended not so much to describe the structures themselves, but rather to give a general idea of the circumstances under which architecture is made in this city.

As with all cities, there appear to be significant moments in history which have contributed to the creation of Montréal's image. In the 1960s, the 'Quiet Revolution' witnessed the rise of nationalism in Québec. Although there was a consolidation of the Québecois identity, the possibility of the province's separation from Canada led to much of Montréal's wealth being sent on its way to Toronto, an effect that has led to periods of stagnation and delays in the development of the urban fabric. While the politicians actively encourage investment from overseas, they continue to install and enforce a system of linguistic apartheid in a culture admired internationally for its bilingualism. Although there is evidence to suggest that architecture is capable of expressing nationalism, to what extent it has been employed in this capacity in Montréal I am still not sure. Having thrashed out the pros and cons of devolution in a slew of recent referenda, many Montréalers confessed to being simply too exhausted with the issue to offer an opinion on whether architecture had any influence upon politics. At the time of writing this book, however, a raging debate was taking place over the siting of a new library. The boulevard St-Laurent is a perceived axis between Francophone and Anglophone cultures, and many feel that plans to position yet another significant civic resource on the west and historically Anglo side would only aggravate an already unrepresentative distribution.

The World Exposition in 1967 and the Olympic Games in 1976 are two further moments in recent history that have contributed significantly to Montréal's international profile, events which showcased the city's engagement with the contemporary debate on architecture and urbanism. Several of the structures built for these events are still there and serve as a fascinating testament to the design ambitions of their respective periods. Thanks to recent work undertaken, some of the projects are featured in this book, notably the United States pavilion which has been transformed into an ecology centre (see page 154) and the French pavilion which is now a casino (page 156). Many local architectural practices benefited from the cross-fertilisation of ideas that are implicit in the staging of such major international events, and new lines of enquiry were established which would influence the design community and are still being investigated today.

The awarding of prizes has become the predominant means by which the public is made aware of local architectural issues. Increasingly concerned about the way in which their city evolves, community and special interest groups now constitute a vocal presence which has made significant improvements to the consultation process, as evidenced by the Little Burgundy Sports Centre by Saia et Barbarese (see page 132). Such beneficial collaboration with the public is strangely contrasted by the non-codified silence among the architects themselves.

SW There seems to have been a long period of silence in Montreal?

Ricardo Castro (architectural theoretician) The aspect that I think is problematic is the lack of critical activity. This type of 'silence' is created by the fact that architects don't talk about the work of other architects. If you are a member of the Ordre des Architectes (of Québec) it is considered unethical to evaluate in critical terms. Here, you don't rock the boat. There is, however, a certain critical effort; I wouldn't say that one must discard everything. You have the competitions, you have the 'Prix d'excellence' in which people are submitting their work and are being evaluated critically by a group, but it is a group that has been certified. They are judges, therefore they can choose; they can say, although they don't say too much, too often.

One hotbed of critical activity concerns the preservation of Montréal's architectural heritage. Much of the building currently taking place involves the recycling or renovation of existing buildings, and over 30 per cent of the projects included in this guide deal with some aspect of conservation. Since the demolition of the Van Horne Mansion in 1973 there has been a concerted effort to limit the destruction of architectural fabric, both modern and antique. Led by Sauvons Montréal, the movement has met with considerable success in the ongoing fight against the wrecker's ball. This group is now turning its attention to criticising new work, and has devised its own awards system through which it publicly applauds or chastises recent projects. The Orange prize is awarded for work deemed as sympathetic to the general well-being of the architectural vernacular, and the Lemon prize for work which is not. Projects mentioned in this book that have received the former are the CCA Garden (page 66), Le Val de l'Anse (page 290), Pointe-à-Callière Musée d'Archéologie et d'Histoire de Montréal (page 32), Musée McCord (page 88), IBM-Marathon Tower (page 50), Old Port redevelopment (page 38), Espace Go (page 210) and Usine C (page 182). Lemons were received by 1000 de la Gauchetière (page 48) and the HEC (page 246).

SW Is there any abuse of these awards?

Odile Hénault (architectural critic) My personal view is yes. Years ago, when Sauvons Montréal started giving out the Oranges and Lemons, it was fun, and was probably the one awards programme that people would look forward to reading about in the newspapers. It had an element of blame associated with it, and controversy is always popular. In recent years, however, the public has become bemused. For example, one year two high-rises got the awards: the IBM Marathon tower was awarded the Prix Orange while 1000 de la Gauchetière got the Lemon. The public couldn't figure it out, and not much was done to explain the decision to them. By giving a Lemon award to the HEC, which is a brave and intriguing building, the organisers discredited themselves completely. This is unfortunate, because the awards programme could be a tool to promote better architecture. Instead it has become a knife in the hands of a small circle of friends closely linked to Heritage Montréal, which is one of the most powerful lobbies in the city. The power that such a tool holds should be used more wisely. Less incestuous jury panels would help. As far as the architects themselves are concerned, the Ordre des Architectes' award is still held in much higher esteem and the most coveted award is of course the Governor General's.

Also worthy of note is the Ministry of Culture's policy for the integration of art into architecture. Since 1981, any public building with a budget of $150,000 or more must set aside 1 per cent of the construction cost for the integration of a work of art. A commitee composed of representatives of the client, two specialists in the visual arts, a representative from the Ministry of Culture and the architects themselves evaluate the artworks proposed by local artists, and select a project to be integrated. Some 1300 artworks have been commissioned and subsequently realised under the scheme.

SW Do the architects feel that the policy of putting 1 per cent of a project's budget into art implies that the architect's contribution is not classed as artistic? Is it possible that someone is enforcing a clear distinction?

Ricardo Castro I guess there is a certain split, or schism, between what goes on in art and what goes on in building. I would imagine that architects like Atelier Big City would argue along the lines that some of their work involves an integration of everything. On the one hand it's good to have support for the 'arts' but it does create a dichotomy in many cases. I would find it a challenge, as an artist, but then one might have to fall into a certain category of artist, those who deal with installations or are involved with in-situ art where this dialogue exists. Some of the projects in Montréal reveal this quality because the artists were more concerned with the site, whereas some others might just bring their work and dump it on the architectural project.

One emphatically Canadian element of Montréal's image is the climate. Climate has a profound impact upon the nature of architectural production. Temperatures in Montréal vary widely from one season to the next, descending as low as -33°C in the winter and climbing to 38 °C in the summer. This influences construction scheduling, life-cycle costing and of course detailing, with thermal gain and loss, extremes of humidity, heavy snow loads and wind-shear forces all taken very seriously as design considerations. A visit to Montréal during the December to February period, when the temperature averages an ear-chiselling -10 °C, is an enlightening experience. I hope that this guide will encourage both architects and non-architects alike to seek out some of the new work – even if it means enduring the occasional bout of inclement weather – and to witness the beginnings of some brave new architecture.

ACKNOWLEDGEMENTS

I would liketo thank the following: the architects and designers who gave so generously of their time and resources; the staff at McGill University, Dave Covo, Ricardo Castro and Avi Friedman; Odile Hénault for the gift of her encyclopaedic knowledge; the staff at the Canadian Centre for Architecture for putting up with my appalling library manners; Jeff and Marta Ware for their continual support work and the wheels; to the Gat Pack for their own particular brand of advice; Cynthia Joy, Carolyn Cooper; and to Seymourina Cruse for letting me breathe from her tank.
SAW, January 1998

Using this book

Montréal is an easy city to navigate because it is based on a loose grid. The projects in this book have been divided into 14 areas which are mostly to be found on the main island and all but one are within the catchment district of the public transport system. Wherever possible I have tried to organise the guide so that the projects grouped together in each area are within walking distance of each other.

Public transport in Montréal is generally very efficient and the Métro is kept impeccably clean. A network of buses fills in the gaps between the underground lines, and there is a system of transfer tickets which enables passengers to change from Métro to bus or from bus to bus without paying an additional fare. The public transport service or STCUM publishes an excellent map which includes the Métro routes and bus lines as well as some of the commuter trains to the suburbs, each with their respective timetables. Where projects are more than a five-minute walk away from the Métro station I have included the bus connection.

Bicycles and in-line skaters are extremely well accommodated, and there are landscaped, serpentine paths which follow the Lachine Canal and the Rivière des Prairies. Ascending Mont-Royal can be quite an effort and even hazardous in winter and it is advisable to go around the hill rather than over it. For trips to the Eastern Townships, a car is *de rigeur.* There are buses which serve the area and the schedules can be obtained by visiting the Voyageur Bus Terminal or by calling 842 2281.

The tourist information centre is located at 1010, rue Ste-Catherine Ouest (Métro Berri/UQAM) and can be reached at 873 2015. I would suggest buying the map of Montréal published by Kukie, which is large enough to include all of the projects except those in the Eastern Townships and the scale shows all of the streets. It is worth remembering that streets are often referred to by their name alone without specifying whether it is a boulevard, avenue or rue (street). The major attractions (the Musée McCord and the Casino for example) are easy to find because there are special blue street signs for tourists dotted around the town.

Old Montréal

Behaviour

This project bears all the marks of an extraordinary relationship between architect and client. Atelier in situ were in fact *in situ* when their warehouse/workshop was targeted for transformation into offices for a multimedia software company. The client set the tone for flexible brief-writing by stipulating that the building accommodate 'as much as it would take'.

The result is a superimposition that flirts with saturation but never gives in to it. The original shell came replete with hard-core industrial fittings, including rolling cranes and hoists. This has all been frozen by a sort of architectural fixative, forcing you to read the new insertions as volumes and independent possibilities rather than the empty moments between industrial relics. It is cause for reflection that the demands of a squeaky-clean high-tech environment should be possible within an ageing shed designed to weld together bits of ships, and the new architecture places itself within that moment of technological transition. The enormous footprint is a rough parallelogram with one side shaved off by the railway and the other slightly bellied out, with the existing internal geometry governed by the need to shift extremely big things in and out. This organisation, a relic in its own right, continues to dictate the primary spatial programme, augmented now by a system of steel catwalks, mezzanines and stairs that have been crafted with a quasi-religious zeal worthy of the shipbuilders.

ADDRESS 10, rue Duke
CLIENT TGR Zone Corporation
STRUCTURAL ENGINEERS Nicolet Chartrand Knoll Ltée
SIZE 5000 square metres COST $6 million
GETTING THERE Métro line 2 to Square-Victoria
ACCESS to lobby

Old Montréal

Atelier in situ 1997

Marché Bonsecours

One of several projects instigated in the build-up to the city's 350th anniversary, the renovation of Marché Bonsecours was undertaken in two phases. Firstly, a dignified restoration of the much-loved historical shell was completed, including an essential fit-up of interiors and services to create four new exhibition spaces. Secondly, a monumental stair was constructed in order to give access to a new upper-level commercial arcade from the rue de la Commune.

All the new structure has been rigorously kept clear of the old, thereby showing its respect. Nowhere is this clearer than in the monumental stair, which appears rickety when set against the original bas-relief portico. The new timber structure feels temporary, like a scaffold erected for the winter only, and in trying to gain altitude within a limited envelope, winds through a series of exhausting turns. Inside the shell, however, the precise new insertions act like a lens through which the old building can be seen in all its pomp and ceremony. The removal of two large wooden doors has allowed an air of transparency to fill the space. 'Noble' materials are to be found throughout: slate, limestone, glass and steel. The interior work by Atelier Big City is refreshingly irreverent (considering the buiding's history as a former home of government) and adds a Simpson-esque colour scheme as well as a lively appropriation of street-light technology which animates the ductwork and creates a sense of procession.

ADDRESS 350, rue St-Paul Est
CLIENT Société Immobilière du Patrimoine Architectural de Montréal
STRUCTURAL ENGINEERS Géniplus SIZE 4000 square metres
COST phase 1: $2.95 million, phase 2: $1.4 million (1996)
GETTING THERE Métro line 2 to Champ-de-Mars
ACCESS open

LeMoyne Lapointe Magne 1992

LeMoyne Lapointe Magne 1992

Chaussegros-de-Lèry

Perched on a ridge as it runs through Vieux-Montréal, the rue Notre-Dame has the ability to thrust any building on its flanks into the skyline. Therein lies the dilemma for this multifunctional complex which yearns for attention with its peaked tower yet is camouflaged into the greyness of its surroundings. Whereas at Point-à-Callière (see page 32) Hanganu had found a sincere poetic link with the historic fabric, here the language is more blatant and straightforward. The project, a large perimeter-block style development, was built in phases. To the west, facing city hall, are municipal offices with the public entrance off the angle under the tower. Inside, the lobby leads to a glazed waiting room from where the slope of the hill falls away, hoisting the ground floor into a raised portico overlooking the lawns of the Champ-de-Mars. The ambience is Gotham City, vaulted spaces suffused with a grey, eerie light. Totems dotted around are inset with colours just warm enough to be distinguished.

Ringing the rest of the block at ground floor are commercial spaces that duck in and out of an arcade. Residential condominiums occupy the upper floors. In contrast to the flat perimeter façade with its forceful detailing, the courtyard within the perimeter benefits from an informal volumetric treatment and features a dramatic split-level garden.

ADDRESS 303, rue Notre-Dame Est
CLIENT Chaussegros, Inc.
ASSOCIATE ARCHITECTS Provencher Roy et Associés, Architectes; Cardinal Hardy et Associés STRUCTURAL ENGINEER Géniplus
SIZE 16,000 square metres with 1100 underground parking spaces
COST $37 million
GETTING THERE Métro line 2 to Champs-de-Mars or Bus 38
ACCESS restricted to City of Montréal service areas

Dan S Hanganu, Architecte 1991

Dan S Hanganu, Architecte 1991

Pavillon Jacques Cartier

Built on the foundations of a demolished warehouse, the Jacques-Cartier pavilion recalls the protracted rythym and linearity of the industrial sheds that had at one time served as the mercantile lungs of Montréal. Forty-two pointed steel masts run the length of the old quay, supported by adjacent steel ribs which provide some structural triangulation. Together, these ribs become the framework for a raised walkway and a large enclosure which is tucked into its lee at the shore-bound end of the axis. Additional structures will be integrated further down the spine as the popularity of the quay grows, which will probably mean fairly soon.

The lateral section offers the most insight into the references at work. Steelwork is kept open wherever possible so that its repetition and modular formula clearly evoke the warehouse theme. The enclosures are outlined by a corresponding series of rectangular frames pinched at the end in a Jean Prouvé manner and reminiscent of travelling hoists. A curved roof has been shaped into a profile which recalls the capsized hull of a Great Laker. Also on a nautical theme is the row of masts, tautly rigged with tension cables in order to support the wooden gangway, though it has also been pointed out that the vanishing points that appear within the constructed perspective are more evocative of grain conveyor belts.

ADDRESS Vieux-Port, opposite the place Jacques-Cartier
CLIENT La Société du Vieux-Port de Montréal
ASSOCIATE ARCHITECTS Les Architectes Simon Cayouette-Lucien Chartrand et Associés
COST $2.6 million
GETTING THERE Métro line 2 to Champ-de-Mars, bus 19, 26, 38 to the Place Jacques-Cartier
ACCESS open

Cardinal Hardy et Associés 1993

Maison des Éclusiers

The assembly is straightforward: vertical planes, a steel lattice and a concrete cylinder are packed tightly around a broad wedge. Spaces derive their character from the tectonic dependencies that exist between the component parts and from the views framed by the placement of each architectural element. The pavilion provides several services. The wedge contains a ground-level café whose clientele is made up largely of in-line skaters, cyclists, and pedestrians seeking refuge from the traffic. Upstairs, in the thick end of the wedge, there is an 'interpretation centre', an informal museum devoted to the history of the Lachine Canal, after whose locks the pavilion is named. Housed within a glazed section of the concrete cylinder is the lockmaster's booth itself, which will be occupied and active once the canal is opened to pleasure craft. The top of the cylinder contains a helical stair that leads up to a belvedere. An imposing steel gantry connects all these together, creating a terrace in its shelter and drawing attention to the awesome spectacle of the silos opposite across the canal.

Whereas the Jacques-Cartier pavilion in the eastern sector of the port evokes the strange contradiction of demolition followed by historical reference, the Maison des Éclusiers is a folly of loose associations, with its casual sequences working on a scale that invites people to make it a place of their own.

ADDRESS Vieux-Port, western sector
CLIENT La Société du Vieux-Port de Montréal
COST $1 million
GETTING THERE Métro line 2 to Square-Victoria, bus 60, 26
ACCESS open

Cardinal Hardy et Associés 1992

Cardinal Hardy et Associés 1992

iSci Centre

The province of Québec is well known for its mega-flea markets and the old King Edward Pier structure used to house one of its finest. Curiosities of the 19th and 20th centuries have now been replaced by those of the 21st, the quay stripped down and refitted with razor-sharp architecture and a mind of its own.

The mind in question is the CTC or Centralized Technical Control, a single brain which monitors most of the building's systems including fire security, heating and ventilation, surveillance cameras, bar-code bracelet ticketing and parking access. Other innovations include lifts that operate using magnetic induction (a small-scale permanent magnet of precious metals installed in the lift shaft rather than overhead) and glass walls silk-screened with a vitrified ceramic coating (reducing entry of sunlight in the summer). The bottom line is that energy efficiency is optimised using intelligent materials and intelligent systems.

The iSci Centre is a showcase for new technologies, and the building's physical transparency echoes the attempt to demystify science and nature. Glass housings for air-conditioning systems help to blur the edges between 'museum' and 'exhibit'. One is caught up in the wonder of blinking diodes and coloured wires. If there is an architectural judgement to be made here, it may be of the kind which downplays conventional beauty and compliments intelligence.

ADDRESS King Edward Pier, Old Port of Montréal (www.isci.ca)
CLIENT La Société du Vieux-Port de Montréal
COST $49 million
GETTING THERE Métro line 2 to Champ-de-Mars or Place d'Armes. Bus 19, 26, 38 to the Place-Jacques-Cartier
ACCESS open every day; call (514) 496-iSci for times

Gauthier, Guité, Daoust, Lestage architectes 2000

Gauthier, Guité, Daoust, Lestage architectes 2000

Notre-Dame bridge building

In response to a familiar scenario of inner-city urban neglect, the municipal administration has undertaken a new large-scale initiative on each of the three flanks of the old city: the Faubourg (suburb) des Récollets to the west, the Faubourg St-Laurent to the north, and the Faubourg Québec to the east.

The eastern ends of cities are renowned for their industrial heritage as well as their general delapidation, and Montréal's is no exception. The 12-hectare site was once a hill, with the ridge of the rue Notre-Dame running eastwards towards Québec City. Steady incursions by the railroad soon undermined the hill, leaving the rue Notre-Dame suspended in the air in the form of a viaduct, spanning the tracks and sheltering a fledgling market beneath its wrought-iron spans.

The project by Dupuis Letourneux is effectively a slickly-updated reproduction of that viaduct across a now barren site from which even the railways have retreated. It is also the first urban gesture towards taming a site that will eventually see 200,000 square metres of housing (both private and social), 20,000 square metres of commercial and 3000 square metres of community-related space built upon its surface by different architects over a period of 12 years. The overall budget has been set at $350 million. At the moment, the planning, site preparation, civic infrastructure and landscaping of the new faubourg are financed by all three levels of government (municipal, provincial and federal) and the private sector. Some 350 units of social housing are to be built with funding from federal and provincial housing agencies, with the remaining 1450 units to be developed by the private sector. First among the architects to complete a housing scheme were Saucier + Perrotte, but their building quickly fell victim to the hazards of turnkey development and is subsequently disappointing. Their half-block will soon become whole,

Dupuis Letourneux, Architectes 1997

Dupuis Letourneux, Architectes 1997

hybridised with another scheme, and so on and so forth. The ability of this new scheme to evolve into a real quartier will be dependent upon the continuation of progressive commissioning and a more sensitive development strategy from the private sector.

Much is expected of the bridge. It will organise the circulation of traffic on the site, re-establishing the north–south axes of St-Hubert, St-André and Amherst. Buildings will grow up next to it, duty-bound to respect a bi-level street frontage. Two magnificent cold storage warehouses will be brought within reach of speculative interests. A new form of insertable-container commercial space, the modern counterpart to the old market, will be sheltered between the abutments. It will offer views of the St Lawrence river and back across to the skyline of Mont-Royal, and has been equipped with an extended promenade, luring strollers off the sidewalk to a hanging pedestrian lay-by. Being both road and roof, it has been assembled with full water protection, and the finish on the concrete exceeds most contemporary standards. The title 'bridge building' is not easily earned considering the profusion of codes to which the structure must conform.

ADDRESS rue Notre-Dame east of rue Berri
CLIENT SHDM and the Service des Travaux Publics, Ville de Montréal
ASSOCIATE ARCHITECTS Saia et Barbarese, Architectes
SIZE 435 metres long by 15 metres wide
COST $9 million
GETTING THERE Métro line 2 to Champ-de-Mars
ACCESS open

Dupuis Letourneux, Architectes 1997

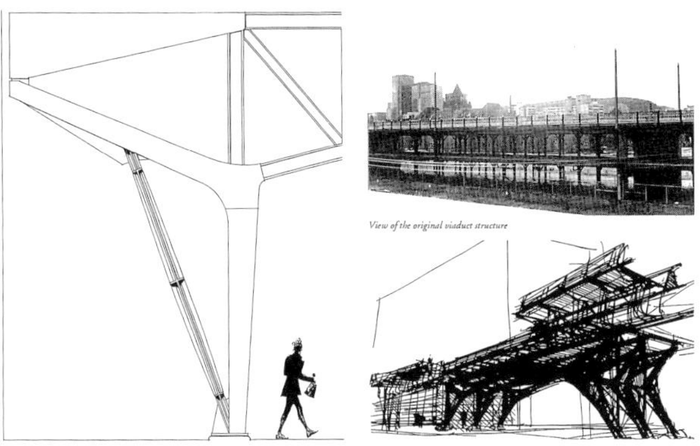
View of the original viaduct structure

Dupuis Letourneux, Architectes 1997

Panique au Faubourg projections

In all, four monochrome images were projected onto the towering silos of the Vieux-Port from the Maison des Éclusiers. The first was a curtain, followed by a row of latter-day caryatids, then a motionless series of waterfalls and, finally, a set of helical stairs. Each image spanned the full height and much of the length of the concrete structure, using it as a screen, encouraging you to reflect upon the personality, scale and presence of those silos.

This is a project that occupies a magical niche. If art and architecture can be differentiated on the grounds that the former offers an alternative reality while the latter must offer a reality, then this project provides both in that it transforms the perceptions of a building via a singular, albeit ephemeral, event. The use of the structure as a screen seems most critical here. The intervention came about as a reaction against plans to demolish the silos, with common public opinion holding that the city would be better off with a clear view across the river ... but to what? Without these structures, many of which have already been torn down, Montréal would lose one of its critical physical delimitations, a bracket around the urban set. As an emphatic urban directive the projections rank with any arguments put forward for maintaining the unbuilt summit of Mont-Royal as the highest point in the city; more provocative still, they expose the role that architecture plays as 'the stageset for future memory'. While the culture of reference holds sway in the city, it is invigorating to discover a project which succeeds in transforming the existing urban fabric through the overlay of an unexpected medium.

ADDRESS Vieux-Port, eastern sector
CLIENT Quartier: 'Éphémère'

Atelier in situ 1997

Atelier in situ 1997

Pointe-à-Callière Musée d'Archéologie et d'Histoire de Montréal

The designers have taken a new look at the idea of the museum and developed an experience of history which combines theatre with artefact. As such, the traditional hierarchy of the museum – containers-within-containers strung together by a loose-fit circulatory system – is replaced by a deliberate and focused choreography. During this sequence, the new architecture (and the bones of its dead ancestors) has been made to point things out, to commentate on the preciousness of things, to appear and disappear, thereby suggesting ways in which architectural presence can affect the understanding of place and memory.

The project links two above-ground structures, one new and one old (the Eperon building and Ancienne Douane, respectively), via an underground tunnel. Guided from the new to the old via the ancient in a scripted sequence, five constituent exhibitions unfold, starting with the multimedia show in the Eperon building, continuing down to the basement, through a rocky subterranean corridor into the archaeological crypt itself, and finally from the basement to the upper floors of the Ancienne Douane. Moving from the heavy, exposed concrete entrance hall down to the archaeological remains below, you marvel at just how lightly the architects were able to bring the building to the ground.

Try to look beyond the obvious programmatic requirements of a site as historically loaded as this one, where respect had to be paid to the morphology of the former Royal Insurance building (including the campanile), the ubiquitous grey limestone had to be employed as the principal façade material, and the archaeological remains were to be left undisturbed. What comes through in this case are inferences of the design method, subtle and powerful because they demand a certain willingness to decipher. The Eperon building, for example, has a façade onto the rue

Dan S Hanganu, Architecte 1992

Dan S Hanganu, Architecte 1992

de la Commune that is so closely shaven that nothing protrudes beyond its plane. The same goes for most of the envelope, which has been treated as though it were too large for the site and has been planed down to fit the footprint. I took this to be evocative of the procedures of masonry. The tower provides a singular point of sculptural release, and fortunately there was no obligation to re-do the clock. There are populist metaphors too, and publications are on sale to help you identify them (for example: metal rods in the tower represent concrete reinforcement bars, implying that history constantly builds on the past).

Dominating the interior of the Ancienne Douane building is the gift shop. It takes a good eye to spot the architecture here, which is almost entirely occluded by tourist paraphernalia, but it is possible to see how the old stone shell has been gutted and refitted with sculpted insertions. Outside, the excavations have been covered by a raised square (also by Hanganu) which features a narrow crack of glazing that draws attention to the treasures on show beneath the surface.

ADDRESS 350, place Royale (musee-Pointe-a-Calliere.qc.ca)
CLIENT SIMPA, Inc.
ASSOCIATE ARCHITECTS Provencher Roy et Associés, Architectes
CONSULTING ARCHITECT (Ancienne Douane) LeMoyne Lapointe Magne
STRUCTURAL ENGINEER Nicolet Chartrand Knoll Ltée
SIZE 6,93135 square metres COST $13.5 million
GETTING THERE Métro line 2 to Place d'Armes
ACCESS call 872 9127 for opening times

Dan S Hanganu, Architecte 1992

Dan S Hanganu, Architecte 1992

Tropiques Nord condominiums

Just imagine what it might have looked like: the original plan dreamed up by the visionary developer Jean de Brabant was for an apartment building entirely covered by a glazed dome. Bylaws governing the control of air intervened, however, and the project was reduced to an atrium a mere 1835 square metres in size. By the time the project had fallen into the hands of the architects, several condominiums had already been sold.

An L-shaped plan has been used to create a southeast-facing enclosure, and it is here that the vast transparent wall has been erected. Rising up 12 floors, it is primarily a system of steel columns supporting inclined trusses built up from hollow sections. Upon this framework is hung the curtain wall whose glass panels vary in specificity according to safety factors and the interior plants' need for a broad energy spectrum of light. Landscaping is reminiscent of the early Tarzan sets, with lots of false jungle watercourses designed and executed by an ex-Disney team. Each of the apartments has a deep terrace which gives onto the tropical garden below. Planters double as concrete upstands and help to reduce the clutter, conveying a sense of anonymity to the façade.

It is interesting to compare this somewhat myopic vision of luxury with Moshe Safdie's Habitat, next door at number 2700. Both share one thing though: they are immensely popular with the residents.

ADDRESS 2500, avenue Pierre-Dupuy
CLIENT Tropiques Nord 1 Montréal Inc.
LANDSCAPE ARCHITECT Ron Williams and Associates
SIZE 31,915 square metres COST $20 million
GETTING THERE bus 168, followed by a 15-minute walk eastwards on avenue Pierre Dupuy
ACCESS none

Tolchinsky & Goodz Architects 1989

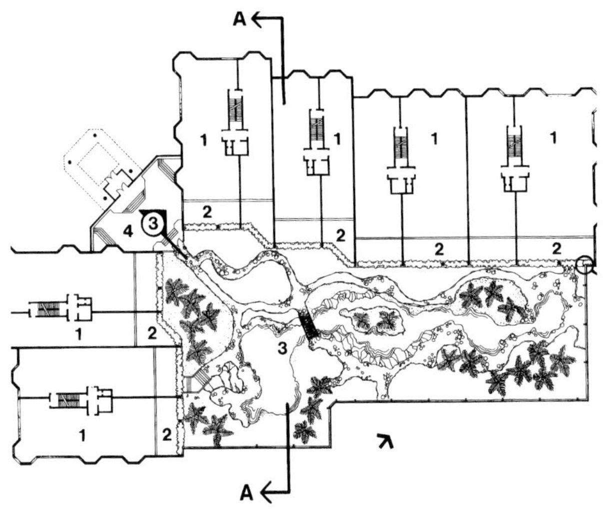

Tolchinsky & Goodz Architects 1989

Vieux-Port redevelopment

One of the true pleasures of visiting a park lies in the tacit acceptance that you will be drawn into a world of considered routes and calculated pauses which anticipate the rhythm of your leisure. The project to redevelop Montréal's old port amounts to the creation of a park in the old-fashioned, philanthropic sense.

The site occupies some 53 hectares of derelict industrial property stretching out along a 5-kilometre band of waterline, with great concrete piers reaching out like fingers to grasp the trade on the St Lawrence river. There are two areas where the new work has been concentrated: a 17-hectare portion to the east which is flat and composed largely of disused quays, and a 12-hectare portion to the west, bisected by the locks that begin the Lachine Canal and therefore blessed with gentle gradients. The sharply defined greystone perimeter of old Montréal provides a uniform northern limit to the site, while to the south there is the St Lawrence river itself and the distant Île-Ste-Hélène, the site of Expo '67.

Much of the design work follows the process of archaeology, and traces of the port's activity that date back to 1825 have been uncovered and integrated into the landscape. Railway tracks were cleared and pieces of cast iron machinery unearthed where the infamous Silo No. 2 had once stood. Both the Lachine Canal and the Bonsecours Basin were excavated and their stone edges restored. Water levels were adjusted in order to create a sense of the water being invited back to the doorstep of the city. The park is read as a densely textured overlay of evolving industry upon which this project forms only a minor film. Connecting bridges were built to link quays to islands, and the east and west sectors were each given a new multi-purpose pavilion. Lighting systems bring the concrete silos into the ensemble by night and points of light pick out the lines of the piers in blue like an airport runway.

Cardinal Hardy et Associés 1992

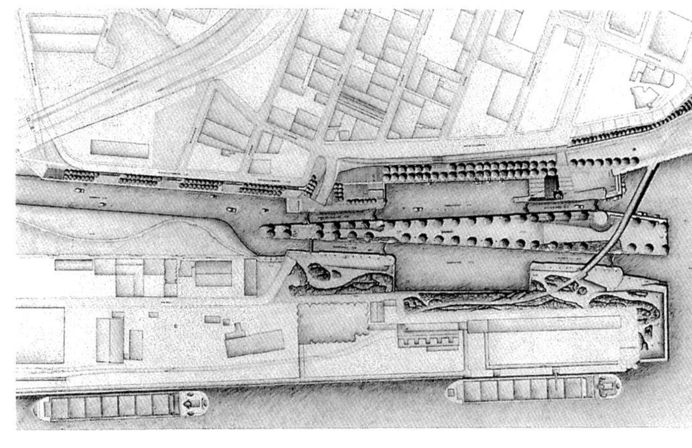

Cardinal Hardy et Associés 1992

The idea of replacing the port with a modern urban park is too obvious to be debatable because the necessity to retain this critical historical element overwhelms any alternative visions for the site. The contemporary aspect of this project lies in the anticipation of how it is used and experienced. This is a park that receives over 3 million visitors a year. Many people who frequent the park do not limit themselves to walking: modern park users are in-line skaters and cyclists, and the pathways, even at peak periods, acknowledge and even encourage such activity. The Lachine Canal itself has been developed as a major thoroughfare for people on wheels, and so the old port becomes part of that continuity. The scale of industry that characterises the port is well suited to the greater distances covered by modern leisure-seekers and so there are different experiences for different speeds.

CLIENT La Sociéte du Vieux-Port de Montréal, Ministère des Travaux Publics de Canada
ASSOCIATE ARCHITECTS Peter Rose Architectes; Jodoin Lamarre Pratte et Associés
DESIGN COLLABORATION Alex Krieger Architect
LIGHTING George Sexton Associates
LANDSCAPE Peter Walker and Partners
SIZE 53 hectares, 29.5 hectares developed
COST $65 million
GETTING THERE Métro line 2 to Place d'Armes or Champ-de-Mars, or bus 26
ACCESS open

Cardinal Hardy et Associés 1992

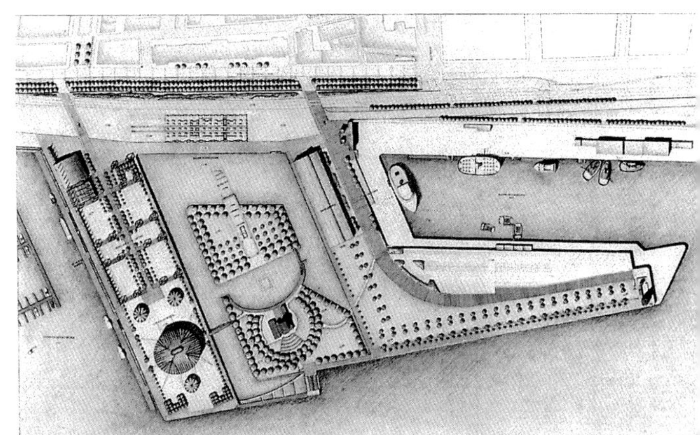

Cardinal Hardy et Associés 1992

World Trade Centre

Occupying an entire block on the edge of Vieux-Montréal, this is one of 80 similar projects worldwide. The task was to reorganise the programming for a dense cluster of 11 buildings, each from a different period. This meant the collaboration of groups from both the private and public sector. In physical terms it required the integration of several different circulation systems and the upgrading of office space.

Creation of user-friendly public space is paramount in such developments. The labyrinth of alleyways and lightwells common to perimeter blocks like these are glazed in and messy mechanical apparatus re-routed. Outside is made inside. We start to lose our sense of what building envelopes are all about, because those highly evolved thresholds become museum pieces. Our imagination is still trying to deal with the museum effect – how to relate to an object that has been removed from its context.

Urban space in Montréal is undergoing this transformation at a rapid rate, often stripping the architecture of its action, and slowly, therefore, its legibility. What we get is something that belongs far more to the sampling generation – a sequence of design decisions whose composition no longer attempts to acknowledge the roots of the source material but aims instead for a new access to the senses.

ADDRESS 393, rue St-Jacques
CLIENT La Société de Promotion du Centre du Commerce Mondial du Montréal Inc.
CONSULTING ARCHITECT Julia Gersowitz
STRUCTURAL ENGINEERS Nicolet Chartrand Knoll Ltée
COST $134.5 million
GETTING THERE Métro line 2 to Square-Victoria
ACCESS to main atrium

Provencher Roy et Associés, Architctes, Arcop Associés 1991

Provencher Roy et Associés, Architctes, Arcop Associés 1991

Downtown

1000 de la Gauchetière

One of the last buildings to be signed by the late Dimitri Dimakopoulos, this 51-storey tower has usurped Place Ville-Marie's role as most identifiable marker on the city skyline. With the territory come the Prince Charles-isms and references to milk cartons or a phallus. Its mannerist attire marks a departure from the purism that has governed most earlier high-rises. Here the podium base, trunk and crown are unified by a deep divisional cleft that acts as a directional beacon. Compositional devices are proferred as foils against the movement to prevent further high-rise development downtown. The podium base centres the building on the axis of Cathédral Marie-Reine-du-Monde, framing it in a large atrium window. 'No one can accuse us of any disrespect for the cathedral,' said Dimakopoulos. Material selection – polished granite cladding and a copper roof – seems to have been informed by a similar lack of disrespect.

Within the atrium there are the obligatory water features and power staircases, but the big surprise is a lively skating rink, open all year round. For the investor or businessman, there are inducements of a more sober nature, not least the availability of large surfaces of up-to-date office space in a downtown core that is unlikely to see investors putting up the money for another tower.

ADDRESS 1000, rue de la Gauchetière
CLIENTS Prodevco Lavelin; Bell Canada Enterprises Development; Téléglobe Inc.; Brookfield Development Corporation
ASSOCIATE ARCHITECTS Lemay et Associés
SIZE 100,000 square metres of lettable office space; underground parking for 650 cars COST $160 million
GETTING THERE Métro line 2 to Bonaventure
ACCESS to concourse levels within podium during office hours

Dimakopoulos and Associates 1991

IBM-Marathon Tower

Kohn Pedersen Fox join an elite group of foreign architects – including Pier Luigi Nervi, Mies van der Rohe and Ieoh Ming Pei – who at various times have added their signatures to the local high-rise movement. It is interesting to note that when local, or even Canadian, architects have attempted to do the same, their efforts are universally lambasted. Much has to do with the increased budget made available when a foreign architect is brought in, but still more has to do with experience. With the tower at 1250 René-Lévesque there is an over-riding sense of coherence, an understanding that this team really knows how to make big buildings. In purely material terms, there is hardly a detail out of place.

There are two entrances, both extremely large – six storeys high to be exact. The first is a bamboo-filled atrium which brings you directly off the street into the serenity of black Peribonka granite and conditioned air. There is a restaurant with a full series of champagne bottles from fillette to jeroboam on display. Volumetrically, the atrium helps to break up the verticality of the tower by adding to the L-shaped plan of the podium base, and the detailing is festooned with art deco, acknowledging the popularity of the style in Montréal. Moving on past the black granite water feature to the monumental reception area, a second grand entrance, you find a busy but nevertheless bleak transition zone linking the service core with the Métro stations and providing views outwards to the landscaped forecourt. Its gentle bay is the most visible trademark of the architects and is used to good effect to focus the plan on the Cathédral Marie-Reine-du-Monde, from several floors up at least. The 47-storey-high tower, clad in vertical strips of Rockville white granite, is peaked with a visor which directs its gaze down to the St Lawrence river to the south and is accompanied by a mast which thrusts a finger towards the sky. We're Number One.

Kohn Pedersen Fox Associates 1992

Kohn Pedersen Fox Associates 1992

The architects have offered this: 'Here we had an opportunity to develop an abstract and integrated tectonic vocabulary which is at once explicitly urbane in its relationship to Montréal and highly reflexive of its object: nature.' Where this project differs from those completed by other foreign 'stars' is that the design follows the same procedure of referentialism that awaits any architect who now deigns to intervene in the downtown area. Beginning with an examination of the vernacular fabric, the project ends with the translation of historical content into an architecture of commemoration, of spectacle. Neither history nor the vernacular is done any great service. The protection of a national or provincial heritage becomes a mission.

ADDRESS 1250, boulevard René-Lévesque
ARCHITECT OF RECORD Larose Petrucci Associates
CLIENT La Société Immobilière Marathon Ltée and IBM Canada Ltd
STRUCTURAL ENGINEER LeMessurier Consultants; Pasquin, St-Jean & Associés
URBAN DESIGN Cardinal Hardy Lestage
SIZE 153,000 square metres
COST $161 million
GETTING THERE Métro line 2 to Bonaventure
ACCESS to lobbies and restaurant

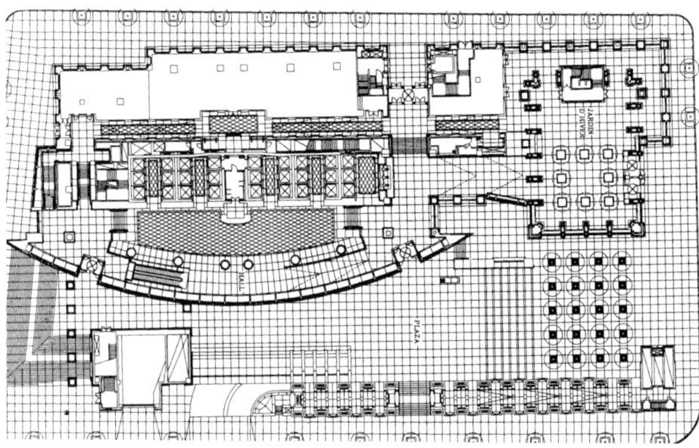

Kohn Pedersen Fox Associates 1992

1801, boulevard de Maisonneuve Ouest

This firm have become masters at blending several seemingly immiscible programmes into one coherent building. Adopting a speculative project with planning permission already granted and a strict set of prescriptions, they have taken a classical, tripartite approach to the composition – a sculpted podium base supporting a lightly-textured body which rises up to the well-proportioned crown. Four three-storey volumes projecting from the façade pick up the scale of a neighbouring terraced row that descends from the rue St-Mathieu. The building thrusts its lower profile forward to the sidewalk, only to retreat once again at ground level to provide a sheltered arcade. The principal façade, composed of yellow, oversized bricks, is segmented vertically by the use of two different fenestration patterns. This division comes to ground on the boulevard de Maisonneuve, where the Métro draws in its clientele to one side and the office workers enter to the other. A conscientious materiality is further accentuated by varnished sheets of perforated metal that dress the entrances to the shops, concrete columns and internal walls.

As part of a growing movement towards design-and-build, the project stands out as a financial success – the architects brought the building to completion with a saving of $400,000. It has also met with critical acclaim. Genteel in proportion and rescued from anonymity by its flying roof, it slips comfortably into the city fabric – an expression of that most highly praised architectural virtue in Montréal: modesty.

ADDRESS 1801, boulevard de Maisonneuve Ouest
CLIENT La Corporation Première Québec/Solim
SIZE 7280 square metres COST $4.5 million
GETTING THERE Métro line 1 to Guy/Concordia
ACCESS to shops and Métro

LeMoyne Lapointe Magne 1993

LeMoyne Lapointe Magne 1993

1501, avenue McGill College

WZMH are a firm with a reputation for letting young designers have a stylistic crack. Their first major commission came in the 1970s in the form of a new External Affairs building in Ottawa, and for a while they were the largest corporate office in Canada. The late- and post-modern styling of their recent towers in Montréal – including the Maison des Coopérants (see page 86), and the crystalline Banque Nationale de Paris building further up on McGill College – has led to allegations that they are performing a kind of absentee architecture, criticism that is undoubtedly fuelled by the cultural feud between Toronto and Montréal.

1501 McGill College answers a lot of those accusations. The first six floors of frame were supplied by Fichten and Soiferman as part of Le Centre Eaton next door, although the architectural treatment was left to WZMH, who had also pioneered the use of air rights legislation. Technically speaking, the upper floors of offices are condominiums. The art deco feel is consistent throughout and the pared-down lobby is refreshingly free of glamorous features, making you feel this can be taken seriously as a place of work. The ziggurat roofline was inspired by the Royal Bank building on rue St-Jaques and is the most powerful assertion of form, although a switch in city officials during the tower's design almost left it flat-topped. Illuminated finials and horizontals now draw attention to the unusual, stepped profile at night.

ADDRESS 1501, avenue McGill-College
CLIENT Polaris Realty
STRUCTURAL ENGINEER Quinn Dressel Associates
SIZE 45,000 square metres COST $45 million
GETTING THERE Métro line 1 to McGill
ACCESS to lobby

Webb Zerafa Menkès & Housden 1991

Webb Zerafa Menkès & Housden 1991

500, rue Sherbrooke Ouest

Heritage Montréal pronounced the original 1982 glass monolith one of the city's ten worst buildings. Located on a gentle inflection of the ultra-prestigious rue Sherbrooke, it had neither the formal attire required to fit in with the crowd nor the presence necessary to make it a serious contender on the real estate market. The colourful pergolas and other adornments that we now see are the response to this image crisis.

Several problems were tackled simultaneously, mostly focused on the underdesigned access from rue Sherbrooke and avenue du Président-Kennedy. The architects held an in-house competition and the winner was a simplistic response which suggested drawing attention away from the original building rather than trying to mess with it. As a result, the entrances are now announced by several colourful follies that obey the orthogonal rules of the incumbent site plan while introducing a scale and style more conducive to street-level identification. The Fisher-Price palette can be offputing when set against rue Sherbrooke's limestone and granite, but it makes sense on the side of the building which overlooks the avenue du Président-Kennedy, where the context is truly severe. The largest of the new pergolas has been built here, inviting you to make a rather daunting climb up two flights of stairs to the piazza, which is such a non-place that it borders on the surreal. The mirrored curtain wall has been used to double-up the new structures, while interaction with the street is restricted to the sound of traffic which echoes off the concrete towers all around, interspersed now and then by a disoriented scream.

ADDRESS 500, rue Sherbrooke Ouest
CLIENT SITQ
COST $6.3 million GETTING THERE Métro line 1 to McGill
ACCESS to lobbies and terraces at lower levels

Blouin et Associés 1986

Blouin et Associés 1986

Aylmer residence

The old red brick of this Victorian family house has been lovingly reconstituted to form three new apartments. With the unusual placement of objects like concrete lintels, the unpretentious unity of the whole suggests an architect functioning effectively as both pedagogue and *bricoleur savant*. According to Lemieux, there are three operative orders at work here: urban, domestic and narrative.

Urban describes the manner in which the secondary façade has been opened up – with new windows and an entrance on the side – to allow for a more efficient use of the corner site. Two large, glazed bays on the ground floor backlight internal staircases and prevent the brick surface from becoming too austere. Domestic explains the expression of the interior composition through the façade; seen from Lorne Crescent, the building can be clearly read as two approximately symmetrical maisonettes with the large ground-floor windows flanking the new side entrance which is central to the axis of symmetry for all the apartments. A very different fenestration system defines the top floor, where a series of punched rectangles provides a steady rhythm of windows and doors along the length of the building and around the corner at either end. Narrative informs the relationship between the curvilinear plan of the new top floor with respect to the contours of Mont-Royal, upon whose shoulder the building sits. The suggestion is that the house, traditionally rectilinear in the time-honoured tradition, is entering a dialogue with the landscape that was silenced by the nature of its implantation.

ADDRESS 3641, rue Aylmer
CLIENT Les Belles Plaisances Inc.
SIZE 3 units, each approximately 60 metres square COST $290,000
GETTING THERE Métro line 1 to McGill ACCESS none

Louis-Paul Lemieux, L'Atelier KAOS 1989

Louis-Paul Lemieux, L'Atelier KAOS 1989

Centre Canadien d'Architecture

Probably the most tasteful example of post-modernism that I have yet to come across, the CCA is the result of a personal and scholarly study of Montréal's architectural heritage, into which is woven an eclectic mixture of themes and investigations that draw upon a panorama of traditions from Sir John Soane to Mies van der Rohe. It was pointed out to me with some chagrin that the choice of architect was not made through the competition process but via the convergence of similar fields of interest. While this has brought about a satisfying coherence in the application of a design strategy, it has made for an introverted building, an architecture that is more interesting as a process than as a product. The CCA has published an enlightening book, *Canadian Centre for Architecture: Buildings and Gardens* (ed. Larry Richards, Montréal 1992) which helps to position the project and its authors with respect to the wider architectural discourse.

Such issues aside, the building is a powerful presence upon the site and the technical achievement within is astounding. What you see is only the tip of the iceberg. Housing an enormous collection of sensitive material, the internal environment of this museum-cum-treasury is rigidly controlled and the sealing process is brought to your attention immediately via three successive front doors. Humidity, temperature and light are strictly modulated throughout. Only the 18th-century Shaughnessy House remains unsealed. In the exhibition rooms and halls the natural light is subtly invited in from above to augment the sense of progression, while on the lower-ground level the natural light is deployed from the façade with great determination to reach the administrative offices. The dictates of access, security, fire protection and electronic systems all combined to inform the design of a building which is at once laboratory, office and public gallery. Facilities to which the public has access include

Peter Rose 1989

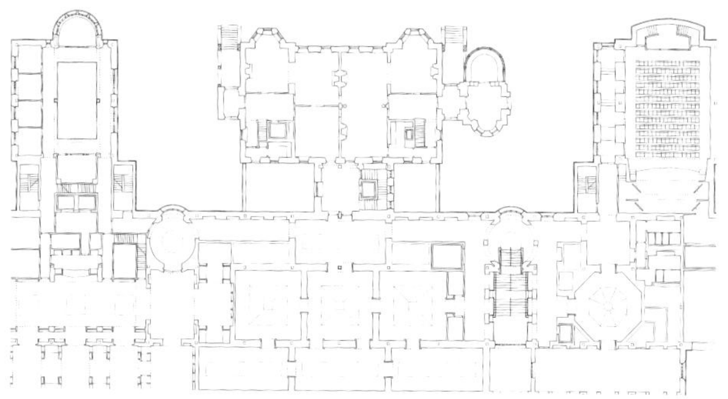

Peter Rose 1989

an auditorium (with extraordinary maple panelling), a bookshop, galleries and a scholars' library. The quality of detailing alone is indicative of the high standards and no-expense-spared attitude brought to the design of the building, with 100 years considered as the minimum lifetime for many of its components.

Together with the Pointe-à-Callière Musée d'Archéologie et d'Histoire by Dan S Hanganu (see page 32), the CCA building appears to have inherited the mantle once worn by the Maison Alcan as the protagonist of new architecture in Montréal, and it is hoped that the qualified approach to design which it broadcasts will be matched by projects which break the rules with equal devotion.

ADDRESS 1920, rue Baile
CLIENT Canadian Centre for Architecture; director, Phyllis Lambert
CONSULTING ARCHITECT Phyllis Lambert
ASSOCIATE ARCHITECT Erol Argun
STRUCTURAL ENGINEERS Nicolet Chartrand Knoll Ltée
SIZE new building: 12,132 square metres;
Shaughnessy House: 1800 square metres
COST $48 million
GETTING THERE Métro line 1 to Atwater or Guy-Concordia;
bus 150, 15
ACCESS to exhibitions and bookshop, other facilities by appointment only. Call 939 7026 for opening times

Peter Rose 1989

CCA Garden

Opposite the Canadian Centre for Architecture there was a derelict strip of land, the result of demolition necessary in order to construct the autoroute Ville-Marie in the mid 1960s. It has been transformed into a garden, rich in its layering of metaphor and popular in its appropriation by scholars, fashion photographers and newly-weds.

Melvin Charney Doing work like this is like 'building'; it's a very long process.
SW There's a tremendous depth to your strategy here. Does it worry you that it probably goes over people's heads?
Melvin Charney It doesn't. I try to aim at the top and the bottom of the social scale and allow others to take care of themselves. The trouble one usually has is with those who follow an introductory course in art and assume they know what they like and dislike. People at the popular end seem to assimilate the work with ease, perhaps because its resembles portraiture – they *see* it as it is.

The idea was to block off the view to the horizon from the street by building up the land, tilting it forward so that you can see the garden both in plan and elevation, and so that people going by in a car can grasp its outline at a glance. It is also titled up for safety's sake; you can see the whole garden from the street except for a narrow section behind the arcade. The horizon reappears once you are on the esplanade of the garden.

There is a plaque next to the road which gives a detailed description of the layout, from the allegorical columns to the planting. It is worth reading, although it does not help to decipher the complexity of intellectual thought that the garden offers up.

Melvin Charney 1990

Melvin Charney 1990

Melvin Charney Everything is worked through, not so much in a narrative fashion but in respect of the idea that at the end of the 20th century the post-minimalist tendency in the arts signified a deepening concern with the fact that we are so invaded by images that even non-representationality has also become representational.

SW So you're moving against that immediacy of representation; it's not designed to be 'got' all at once?

Melvin Charney It's not that I'm into being referential and looking into the past, but the only way I can respond to what I see is by confronting directly the mechanisms of representation. One has an intelligence and an eye nurtured since childhood and founded on visual formations and a syntax that we did not invent but have to use to say things about relationships that we are supposed to cope with at the end of the 20th century. Our enunciation, at best, only approximates life. We say the sun rises when we know the earth rotates around the sun. We talk about a trunk on a car because there used to be an actual trunk welded on to its body. And if one is rendered conscious of these archaisms one may trip into something new. To me, what is most important is that the garden, which picks up on every garden ever built – or tries to – is seen to be unercut by and exist in conflict with the expressway.

ADDRESS boulevard René-Lévesque, opposite the CCA at 1920, rue Baile
CLIENT Canadian Centre for Architecture
CONSULTING ARCHITECT Phyllis Lambert
SIZE 5 hectares COST $2.2 million
GETTING THERE Métro line 1 to Atwater or Guy-Concordia;
BUS 150, 15
ACCESS open dawn until dusk

Melvin Charney 1990

Concordia University library

Having done battle with sitting tennants for several years, Concordia University have at long last built their downtown library. It now occupies the better part of a city block, wrapping itself around the former Royal George Conciergerie. This 1912 building was the most profound influence on the library's plan, becoming the centre of its east–west axis of symmetry. The massing was shifted so that most of the new structure is kept well way from the old. Stylistically, the architects opted for a modular construction system capable of appearing quietly coherent despite the presence of a fussy existing building within its midst.

There is heavy reliance on the square as a compositional device, from the three-dimensional concrete grid down to the cubic, metal light fittings and walls of square glass bricks. An atrium which bisects the building at its thickest section helps to break up the all-pervasive sense of an enclosing grid, and various text-sculptures ooze out into the void.

The Concordia building opposite has been designed with the brutality common to so many modern university buildings. It seems that by using the design of the library, the architects have tried to resolve the awkward heterogeneity of building types at this end of the boulevard. I find their response challenging, but awkward with its Aldo Rossi styling. Public opinion is perhaps summed up by the elderly man who asked as I was taking a photograph: 'Is there something that you find interesting?'

ADDRESS 1400, boulevard de Maisonneuve Ouest
CLIENT Concordia University
ASSOCIATE ARCHITECTS Werleman Guy McMahon
STRUCTURAL ENGINEER Boulva Kadanoff et Associés
COST $52.7 million
GETTING THERE Métro line 1 to Guy-Concordia ACCESS open

Blouin et Associés 1992

Blouin et Associés 1992

Cossette Communication and Marketing

The focal point in the transformation of this undistinguished building is the lobby, where the ground and first floor have been married together to form a double-height entrance. The resulting volume is subsequently worked into four lateral zones: a café, viewing hall, reception and lounge. Saucier likens the treatment of these zones to the sets of Peter Greenaway's *The Cook, the Thief, his Wife and her Lover,* but whereas Greenaway's transitions are abrupt as he pans from room to room, here the edges are made less obvious through a play between things that line up and things that don't, with details used as agile, overlapping editing.

An oversized aluminium soffit squashes light out at the street frontage, aided by a floor threshold of polished black granite. The darkness serves two purposes: firstly, it calls attention to a variety of projected images from Cossette's latest ad campaigns and, secondly, it gives life to the materials on the inside which are left to emit their own glow. There are clubby velour ceilings, red marmoleum floors, and frosted glass doors which turn in finely-milled brass fittings, each of which reveals a softer side through its own luminescent properties. Rejecting the call for a Parisien-style café, the architects chose a deep, narrow dimension derived from the Montréal tradition. Dubbed 'the idea accelerator', it is now full of Arne Jacobsen chairs and the gasps from an overworked espresso machine.

ADDRESS 2100, rue Drummond
CLIENT Cossette Communication and Marketing
STRUCTURAL ENGINEERS Dupont Desleules Associés
SIZE 200 square metres
COST $820,000
GETTING THERE Métro line 1 to Peel
ACCESS to lobby

Saucier + Perrotte, Architectes 1996

Les Cours Mont-Royal

Centred around the expansion and renovation of the anecdotally-rich Hôtel Mont-Royal (Mussolini's henchmen allegedly stayed there), this vast but relatively invisible project spans the better part of a city block. The intention was to bring back the ambience cultivated by the hotel when it was a grand refuge for socialites, with the glamour of high-fashion commerce thrown in to set a suitable tone. The architects have united several glazed-over light wells by cutting out floor slabs on the lower levels to create an energetic labyrinth of up-market boutiques, restaurants and cinemas. All of this can be seen from the offices, hotel rooms and luxury condominiums above. Extensive parking facilities were inserted underneath by means of transfer slabs; when 9 metres of mud was found where there should have been bedrock, a cinema *à l'Egyptien* was installed in the 'found' space.

There are lots of trimmings and dressings to ponder. Toronto designers Yabbu Pushelberg, renowned for their fashionable flourishes, were brought in as consultants for the interior treatments. There are grand sweeping staircases that spiral through the air, granite water features with virtual water, and a suspended installation of flying Easter-Island figureheads (some of whom appear to be whistling). Most intriguing of all is the old hotel lobby which has been left exposed on both sides like a room in an open doll's house.

ADDRESS 1000, boulevard de Maisonneuve
ASSOCIATE ARCHITECTS Yabbu Pushelberg
CLIENT La Société en Commandité Les Cours Mont-Royal
SIZE 100,000 square metres including parking COST $88 million
GETTING THERE Métro line 1 to Peel
ACCESS open for boutiques, restaurants and cinemas

Le Groupe Arcop 1989

Le Groupe Arcop 1989

Le Centre Eaton

The architectural typology of the downtown shopping mall has been applied here without too much of the glitzy excess associated with retail of that nature. Based upon a simple axis that connects rue Ste-Catherine with boulevard de Maisonneuve, the mall is horizontally stratified according to a time-honoured system: food court below grade, cheaper shops on the lower floors, and a gradient of exclusivity as you ascend, culminating in the ultimate of inaccessible shop windows, the cinema. There are underground connections in several directions including a new trajectory towards the Place Ville-Marie in 1993 by Fichten Soiferman. The project was considerably restrained by the presence of existing municipal services under rue Ste-Catherine and rue Cathcart, but was nevertheless successful in opening up more retail space and forging a critical link in the underground system.

The Montréal Centre Eaton, like its downtown Toronto counterpart, is an atrium, in this case crowned by a cruciform steel and glass skylight. Circulation by escalators and a lift is kept to the centre, and is simple and easily navigable. Detailing of internal streetlamps, balustrades and other features is restricted to a uniform British racing green, hovering between tasteful discretion and poverty of imagination, all the while allowing the individuality of shop decoration to show through. The same goes for the external treatment.

ADDRESS 705, rue Ste-Catherine
CLIENT York-Hannover Ltd
SIZE 65,000 square metres; phase 2 by Fichten Soiferman connecting Le Centre Eaton to Place Ville-Marie: 1300 square metres
COST phase 1: \$70 million; phase 2: \$10 million
GETTING THERE Métro line 1 to McGill ACCESS open

Peter Rose with Fichten Soiferman, Architectes 1990

Peter Rose with Fichten Soiferman, Architectes 1990

House for a bibliophile

In Pierre Chareau's Maison de Verre, one's sense of occupation is always challenged by the authority of the furniture-made-architecture. This project focuses on the book-made-architecture, and there is a similar displacement of priorities, of permanence, of the possibilities of impromptu human patterns within a highly-designed space. There are 15,000 books here, and this is a house.

Reduced to a carbonised shell by fire in 1992, the house forms part of a red-brick terrace facing the slope of Mont-Royal. The system of construction, a series of trabeations in stone and wood, provided the architect with an ordering device for the space within. Exposed steel beams painted red define and support an interior court which is lit tangentially by a skylight. This frame supports an immaculately detailed stair that ascends the central court to become a glass catwalk, performing the loadbearing function and subverting the Victorian tendency towards enclosure with a perfidious transparency.

Almost every available surface is a bookshelf, a preference emphasised by dark walls and secondary steel elements. Even the fireplace has been silenced by darkness. The shelves stand out in blond maple, announcing their objectness, and are filled with colourful books. Even the 'residential' quarters, a small rear extension on the upper floor, are not entirely book-free. Edited views through the glass-block wall change the subject momentarily, but the overall impression is of being among books.

ADDRESS 1610, avenue des Pins Ouest
CLIENT Ronald A Javitch Foundation
SIZE 700 square metres COST $750,000
GETTING THERE Métro line 1 to McGill, or bus 144
ACCESS by appointment only

Martin Troy, Architecte 1995

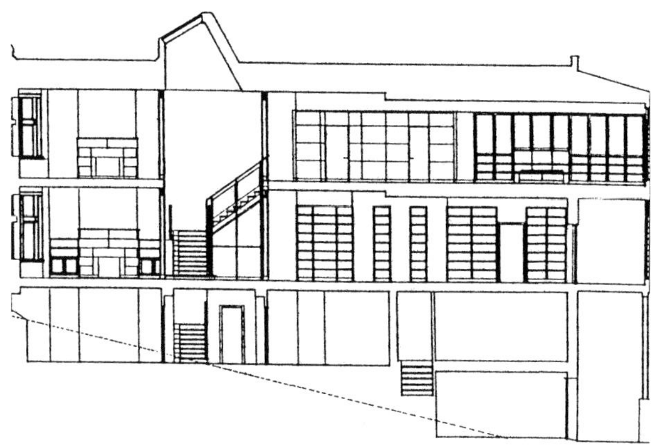

Martin Troy, Architecte 1995

M H Wong Engineering building

With no major building work in almost 30 years, the main campus of McGill was in danger of becoming sacrosanct territory. The successful assimilation of this new member into the club has been achieved through the tasteful crafting and polishing of its façade, upon which a considerable proportion of the intellect has been focused. A primary palette of saturated greys, primarily limestone and anodised aluminium, establishes the immediate contextual reference, followed more whimsically by hanging half-turrets and lead-coated copper shingles. Two main volumes, a foundry and a laboratory block, have been tightly massed around the original Foster radiation building, settling the ensemble comfortably into a site that twists and falls awkwardly.

The dignified face conceals an eccentric mind. The central element of public space and circulation is a void between the existing building and the new laboratories. To enable the unbroken ascent of a four-level staircase, the new concrete frame appears to have been truncated, with prosthetic suspension columns in steel bolted on to stubby protrusions. With flexibility a priority for the functional programme, all services have been left exposed in anticipation of their *ad hoc* appropriation. Descending from the chaotic anatomy of ducts is a most delicate rigging of lights and lenses like visual plumb lines, adding to the mysterious aura of engineers and alchemists working their strange magic together.

ADDRESS McGill University main campus, between Biology Road and avenue Dr Penfield
CLIENT McGill University
ASSOCIATE ARCHITECTS Jodoin Lamarre Pratte et Associés, Architectes
SIZE 14,000 square metres COST 27 million
GETTING THERE Métro line 1 to McGill ACCESS to lobby

Marosi and Troy 1997

Marosi and Troy 1997

Maison Alcan

Those who believe that the golden age of the 45-degree axonometric and aluminium cladding gave us nothing of import should go and see the Alcan headquarters building. The history of the project reads like a list of applaudable decisions more common to the socially-correct 1990s than the early 1980s. The then president of Alcan Aluminium, David Culver, was a man who walked to work at the Place Ville-Marie every morning. Electing to move the headquarters of his multinational company to a site that he had come to know well, Culver chose a series of buildings that fronted onto rue Sherbrooke. On the corner was the Adam-influenced home of Lord Atholstan, a turn-of-the-century work that became an early influence on the Montréal Beaux Arts movement. Further down was the old Berkeley Hotel, which at the time was nervously looking for a new vocation. It was decided that after renovating and recycling, the five original buildings would be linked not to a new skyscraper but to a complex of low-level structures by means of an six-storey atrium to the rear. A bold and human statement had been made.

The emphasis on entry is thus shifted from Sherbrooke to the two side streets by two new wings, although these are practically indistinguishable and share the same grid. Four new entrances weave into an internal circulation that leads to the atrium through an irregular pattern that, although easy to navigate, can be highly deceptive when it comes to searching for an underlying rationale to the plan. Concrete beams are left exposed and patches of granite aggregate warm up the grey of the concrete. Commissioned sculptures extol the qualities of aluminium, and an internal gate by Yves Trudeau, when opened, becomes a shifting game of parallax, its flat bars transformed into 'a jet of liquid metal'. The atrium sets up a six-storey face-off between the aluminium and the brick, and the technologies are so different that they instead complement one another.

Le Groupe Arcop 1983

Le Groupe Arcop 1983

Both inside and out, the cladding presents aluminium at its most seductive. Plenty of tolerance is left between the panels, sometimes up to 25 millimetres, making the proportioning lines seem like mere shadows, absences between the floating plates of skin. Windows turn corners with no awkwardness, sometimes dropping the cill by a few centimetres to acknowledge a change in the plane. Corners are recessed, angled and curved. Vertical lines ascend the façade without fear of being muddled. While the plan is quite restless in its occupation of a complex interstitial site, the building remains cool and utterly confident in its detailing.

The new work is seldom required to be deferential to the old. At the rue Stanley junction the new façade steps back from the building line and the atrium is tucked away and denied the characteristic street presence normally afforded to such hallowed places. Towards the rear, where a right of way has been left open for pedestrians, the neo-Greek form of the Emmanuel Congregational Church is reflected back off the strip windows which are straight and unflinching. With that procession over, the atmosphere becomes quite bucolic with sculptures, atria, wooded areas and pergolas. The pink-brick paving epidemic has won over much of the courtyard and a café has taken up occupancy of the ground floor. One can now sit back and savour the fruits of this civic gesture with the nostalgia of Greece to one side and gracefully redeemed aluminium to the other.

ADDRESS 2100, rue Stanley
CLIENT Alcan Aluminium Ltd
CONSULTING ARCHITECT Julia Gersowitz
COST $43 million GETTING THERE Métro line 1 to Peel
ACCESS to lobby and ground-floor commercial space

Le Groupe Arcop 1983

Maison des Coopérants

The construction of this office tower required a reshuffling of the public square formerly dominated by the Cathédrale Christ Church, part of an ongoing redistribution of architectural material that began in 1927. At that time the 39-metre spire of the neo-gothic church had to be demolished because it weighed too much for its foundations. It was replaced in the 1940s by a steel replica, dressed in aluminium treated to look like the original sandstone.

The new tower by WZMH is not quite so subtle in its adoption of the neo-gothic language. With early occupancy a priority, the dedicated mechanical floor went in at level four, enabling a sort of frieze to be worked into the façade, but the rest is unremarkable and conspicuously apologetic with its mirrored glass in baby-pink tints. The roof is all too easily caricatured. Perhaps it is sufficient to say that if there was respect shown, it was primarily in the painstaking work of plugging the massive tower into a fragile infrastructure. While the tower fast-tracked into the air, urged on by waiting tennants and stiff delay clauses, the presbytery was dismantled stone by stone, reconstructed on the new slab and given an alternative function. The cathedral foundations were excavated and an addition to Montréal's underground shopping concourse eased into place, with a cloister added above to enable access for the general public.

ADDRESS block surrounded by rue Ste-Catherine, rue University, avenue Union and boulevard de Maisonneuve
CLIENT First Cliff
STRUCTURAL ENGINEER Quinn Dressel Associates
SIZE 60,000 square metres COST $50 million
GETTING THERE Métro line 1 to McGill
ACCESS to lobby of office building, cathedral and shopping concourses

Webb Zerafa Menkès & Housden 1988

Webb Zerafa Menkès & Housden 1988

Musée McCord extension

People who know their museums have compared the McCord to the Pitt-Rivers Museum in Oxford, probably because of their scholarly traditions and the idiosyncracy of the collections. I would suggest a similarity through a shared appreciation of fetishism, an attitude that seems to have inspired even the architects who have gone at the detailing with a feverishness that easily matches the collection for originality and obsession.

The original building on Sherbrooke was designed by Percy Erskine Nobbs in 1906 for the McGill student union. It was taken over and converted into a museum in 1967 and, despite the luxurious volumes, was quickly outgrown by the steadily-growing McCord collection. There are costumes, textiles, decorative artworks, paintings, prints, drawings, ethnological artefacts and the extensive photographic archives of William Notman. Significant architectural features, like the vaulted ballroom ceiling, simply disappeared as a result of the 'black box' style of museum organisation prevalent at the time.

The architects have used a new circulatory system to enable a reading of old matched with new. By extending Nobbs' circular plan into a figure of eight, the original floor plate has been continued, making possible lively conversations between the past and present. Spatial sequences revel in the idea of storage, of hiding, enclosing and revealing things by moving around either the visitor or the architecture – the containers and display cases. There are large maple panels which can be swung about to allow open-plan layouts or closed down to encourage a more centrifugal effect. The reception desk was also capable of a limited mobility but has since been replaced. Its track still makes a nice detail.

Materials are critical in achieving the continuity: the floors are green, Burlington slate; the vertical panelling is maple, stained grey or copper; there is volcanic rock; there is glass, either clear, sand-blasted or crackled

J L P et Associés, LeMoyne Lapointe Magne 1989

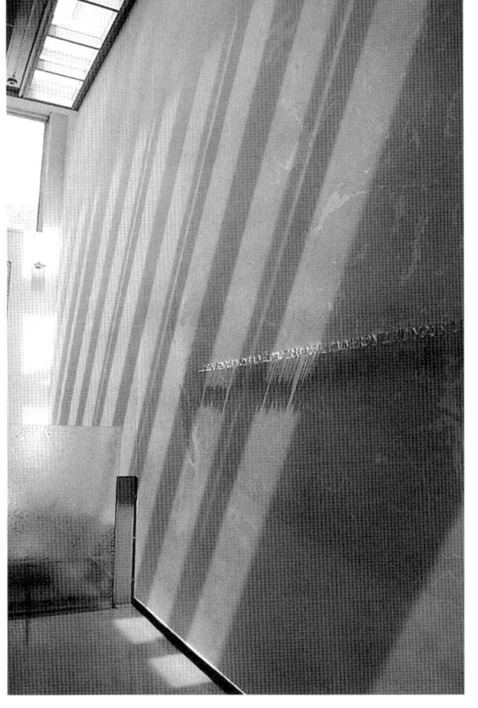

J L P et Associés, LeMoyne Lapointe Magne 1989

with leaf-patterns.

Storage areas and archives are a treasure which the public rarely sees, which is a pity considering the raw strength of an architecture designed to serve the needs of objects rather than those of humans. The McCord's vaults are hidden in the upper levels of the new addition, sealed away behind doors which lock like the hatches of a submarine. Mobile storage walls part like the Red Sea, inviting you down a temporary corridor of shelves and rails. Opening one such drawer, I was unnerved by the sight of several pairs of shoes, tagged and labelled, which seemed unsure of whether to be startled at this disturbance or excited at the possibility of being brought back into the public eye.

ADDRESS 690, rue Sherbrooke Ouest
CLIENT McCord Museum Corporation
STRUCTURAL ENGINEERS Nicolet Chartrand Knoll Ltée
SIZE increased to 9000 square metres
COST $30.5 million
GETTING THERE Métro line 1 to McGill
INTERNET mccord-museum.qc.ca
ACCESS Tuesday to Friday, 10.00–18.00; Saturday and Sunday, 10.00–17.00; closed Monday

J L P et Associés, LeMoyne Lapointe Magne 1989

Molson Center

There are few institutions that can claim to be as close to the heart of local culture as the Montréal Canadiens Ice Hockey Club. Having outgrown their arena on avenue Atwater, the club required premises that were not only larger and more central but also capable of dealing with the modern demands of the sporting industry. The result is an enormous complex which accommodates a breathtaking numer of functions. The arena itself seats 21,500 fans and can also be used as a flexible concert hall for audiences ranging from 2000 to 23,500 people. There are 134 corporate suites, a 170-station press gallery and dedicated press room, 5 ice-level television studios, 3 restaurants, 38 food stands, 7 souvenir stands, 197 cashier posts and a new commuter train terminal. This is only the first phase; there are plans for two adjacent office towers.

Fitting all of this in seems to have been the architects' greatest challenge. The building is a channel for commuters on their way to and from Windsor Station during the day, offering them a broad vista onto the lower flats of St-Henri where some of Montréal's most powerful industrial architecture smokes away in the distance. Enormous trains approach the roofless platforms head-on, pulling up just short of a simple glass wall. The architecture demonstrates a notional fragility that is expressed elsewhere in the building. Bars and restaurants harbour the die-hard fans who can either pick up souvenirs (while watching one of 21 TV screens in the shop) or talk about team politics in the bar (while keeping an eye on the replays on another five large screens). By night, when the big events take place, the interior and exterior public spaces merge and fill to a density that whips up an appropriate crowd mentality without inducing claustrophobia. Inside the arena, the fixed seating is steeply pitched for greater visibility using a system of abacus, precast-concrete bleachers, all roofed over by a beam-string steel structure.

LeMoyne Lapointe Magne 1996

LeMoyne Lapointe Magne 1996

By employing a plurality of scaling mechanisms on the envelope, the architects have demonstrated their consciousness of both the industrial heritage and the irregular, downtown volumetry into which they have insterted their large mass. In order to dematerialise the abrupt façades, they have collaged red brick, limestone, blackened and galvanised metal panels, and the occasional patch of glazing. The personality of each façade varies according to the particular urban condition that it confronts – formal, industrial or social. The building's most remarkable feature faces on to the square that the building now demarcates: a fritted glass curtain wall that seems to cleave its way off the main bulk of the building and thereby leans slightly into the square. Projections from the square can transform the entire wall into a vast screen. This angled glass façade also seems to suggest something else, perhaps a tongue-in-cheek reference to the bravado of hockey itself. Like the perspex screens behind the goal that heave over with the impact of a body check, this sudden break with the orthogonality of the composition suggests both a dynamism and a fragility, as if the building is struggling to contain the explosive atmosphere within it.

ADDRESS 1420–90 rue de la Gauchetière, block bounded by rue Peel, rue St-Antoine, rue de la Montaigne and rue de la Gauchetière
CLIENT Les Consultants du Forum du Canadiens CFC Inc.
ASSOCIATE ARCHITECTS Lemay et Associés
STRUCTURAL ENGINEERS Lalonde, Valois, Lamarre, Valois & Associates; Soprin
SIZE 77,000 square metres
COST $150 million
GETTING THERE Métro line 2 to Bonaventure
ACCESS open

LeMoyne Lapointe Magne 1996

Monument National

The renovation of this much-loved venue amounts to a timely evolution that rescripts its architectural programme for a more contemporary audience. The main theatre was reduced in capacity from 1200 to 800 to improve vision and acoustics, while a new 150-seat self-contained studio theatre was inserted into the bowels of the building, and cloakrooms, dressing rooms, lobbies and a ground-floor café were added.

The building itself is an elaborate affair by Perrault, Mesnard and Venne. Having just celebrated its 100th anniversary, the theatre has managed to retain its lavish detailing both inside and out, which made new attempts at spatial division difficult. Where the new architects have been forced to make enclosures within existing spaces (for the dressing rooms) the effect is inevitably disheartening, and with all the new flytower technology and prop lifts trying hard not to be seen, much of the building has become a labyrinth. Finding your way around backstage is not for those who rely on dead-reckoning navigation. Where the architects have simply added to or replaced the original the effect is positive, like the stainless steel balustrades to the main stair, the semi-mobile kiosk (currently to be found in the zinc and cherrywood café), or the streamlined boxes which have replaced the tubby old baignoires.

ADDRESS 1182, boulevard St-Laurent
CLIENT École Nationale de Théâtre du Canada; administrative director, Simon Brault
ENGINEERS Nicolet Chartrand Knoll Ltée
SIZE 10,000 square metres
COST $19 million
GETTING THERE Métro line 1 to St-Laurent or line 2 to Place d'Armes
ACCESS for performances or by appointment

Blouin et Associés 1993

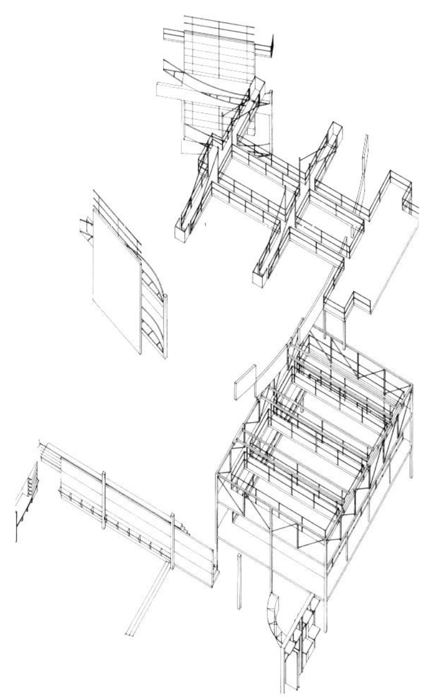

Blouin et Associés 1993

Musée d'Art Contemporain

Having struggled to get by on a former Expo '67 site, the Musée d'Art Contemporain finally saw its chance for a much-needed new building when a location became available on the Place-des-Arts in the prestigious company of the Wilfred Pelletier Hall, the home of the Montréal Symphony Orchestra, the Montréal Opera and the Grands Ballets Canadiens. There was not much space left, however, only a narrow corridor on the westernmost edge of the square, flanked by rue Jeanne-Mance along its entire length from rue Ste-Catherine north to de Maisonneuve. As if to complicate things further, an existing parking facility was to remain below grade. The architects responded with a form that acknowledges the conditions of confinement – a series of planes and pitches running in parallel, with a rotunda announcing the point of contact with the Place-des-Arts itself. Stylistically, the building seems to get little further than schematics, a diagram of Platonic shapes, cosmetic arcades and water courses coloured in with swimming-pool blue. From the outside, the divisive techniques that are intended to humanise the scale by interrupting the section are suspicious in the light of the current spatial demands of contemporary art.

The entrance from Place-des-Arts leads to the reception area, a rotunda device upon which most of the architectural programme depends. It acts as the primary sectional element enabling a helical circulation about its circumference. Most of the floors are serviced from this point, including the café and the main galleries. The rotunda is an effective mechanism which immediately wins your support as a neccessary navigational beacon, but then loses it just as quickly by overcomplicating the geometry. Stairs are hidden away and a vast aedicule in overdistressed copper twists and slays the volume, thereby deflating the spirit with pure artifice. Somehow, the architects have succeeded in maintaining a sense of

Jodoin Lamarre Pratte et Associés, Architectes 1992

Jodoin Lamarre Pratte et Associés, Architectes 1992

progression as you prepare for the art itself. At ground level there is a subterranean feel resulting from the raised deck of the Place-des-Arts outside. Ascending the cylinder of the rotunda, you resurface through the distant ground plane. An axis that faces west syphons the general public off to the galleries, lured by an enormous glazed void which represents their final natural-light experience before being submerged in the exhibition itself. During my visit the gallery skylights had been wrapped Christo-like in material and I was unable to decipher the relationship intended between the natural environment and the works of art, but the open planning and temporary partitioning made for a relaxed circulation that gave each piece of work plenty of room to breath.

The rest of the museum's floor area is either stacked up above or interred below these grand galleries, six upper levels and one lower level in all. The lower level also includes a 250-seat multimedia room which is used for exhibitions, dance performances, theatre, seminars and presentations by artists participating in the exhibitions.

ADDRESS 128, rue Ste-Catherine Ouest
CLIENT Société Immobilière du Québec/Société de la Place-des-Arts
CONSULTING ENGINEER CRS Inc.
SIZE 15,100 square metres
COST $33 million
GETTING THERE Métro line 1 to Place-des-Arts
INTERNET http://Media.MACM.qc.ca
ACCESS call 847 6212 for opening times

Jodoin Lamarre Pratte et Associés, Architectes 1992

Musée des Beaux-Arts de Montréal, Pavillon Desmarais

After the heady success of Habitat in 1967, Moshe Safdie became conspicuously absent from the Montréal scene; some say he was the victim of invidious plotting, others say that you need to go abroad to become really famous. Safdie's belated return saw a string of three major museum commissions in Canada in the space of four years, one of which was this extension to the Musée des Beaux-Arts de Montréal.

Winning the commission was a relatively straightforward procedure in local terms. A panorama of influence was covered by the proposal team of Desnoyers Mercure, Architectes; Lemay Leclerc, Architectes; Moshe Safdie and Associates; and, to strengthen the youthful admixture, Jacques Rousseau, Architecte. Commission in hand, the architects then had to wrestle with the encumbrance of a protected façade which took up half the street frontage on Sherbrooke and a potental building envelope that extended backwards into convoluted alleys and forwards under Sherbrooke to the existing museum. The prestige façade was to have a northern exposure and the rest was to kowtow to several vernacular styles in as many directions.

What has been built has delighted the critics in that it has given them so much to write about. A favourite topic is the front entrance which teeters on that delicate fulcrum between pastiche and reverence. Also popular is the ramp-cum-stair which forces the visitor either to break into a powerstride or to slow to a conversational amble. It is an exercise in re-learning to walk. There are also leaks in the roof, allegedly.

So where has Safdie succeeded? He has managed to bring light to the Sherbrooke façade. The use of light is generally good all around, except where none is available, as in some of the below-grade vaults. Even there he has tried by extending the circulation void. In another glazed atrium

Moshe Safdie, architectural concept 1991

Moshe Safdie, architectural concept 1991

to the rear of the third level the surprisingly generous and rarified atmosphere lets you breath before locking horns with the temporary exhibition. In the picture galleries Safdie has applied a traditional section that served him well in the National Gallery in Ottawa. Circulation can be reassuring as you are always led back to the same place, the entrance lobby. There are a wide variety of spatial experiences: flying walkways, a belvedere and some cosy, out-of-the-way side galleries. Even if the proportions aren't always easily read, the structural geometries impose themselves assertively on the spaces, although you usually have to peer around or notionally remove one conflicting element – a stray horizontal brace, for example – in order to feel that imposition.

With this kind of architecture the museum declares a populist approach toward the general public, and sometimes it is hard to overlook this eventuality. If you consider yourself a purist then you may prefer Arcop's 1976 extension to the Beniah Gibb Pavilion across rue Sherbrooke.

ADDRESS 1379–80, rue Sherbrooke Ouest
CLIENT Musée des Beaux-Arts de Montréal
ASSOCIATE ARCHITECTS Desnoyers, Mercure & Associés; Lemay, Leclerc, Architectes
STRUCTURAL ENGINEERS Dionne, Olechnowicz; Gascon, Vigneault, Dumas; Martineau, Vallée, Régimbald Inc.
SIZE new wing 23,000 square metres COST $95 million
GETTING THERE Métro line 1 to Peel
INTERNET www.mmfa.qc.ca (English)
ACCESS call 285 2000 for opening times

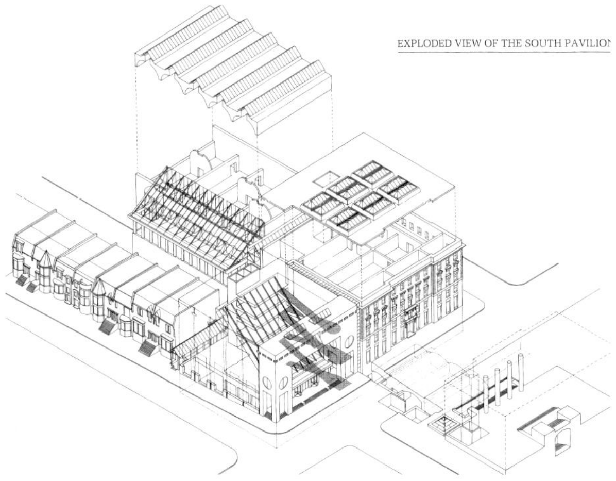

Moshe Safdie, architectural concept 1991

The Next Home™

The Affordable Homes Program was established at McGill University to address the lack of possibilities available to first-time buyers. Rather than indulging themselves in the utopian visions of the avant-garde, the researchers went straight to the building industry and came up with a compact, 4-metre-wide row house dubbed 'the Grow Home'. At $400 per square metre it was nearly half the price of a conventional house. In 1990 a full-scale model was erected on the McGill campus, and within 10 months over 600 units were built in the greater Montréal region.

Then came the Next Home™, based on a larger floor plan and featuring a built-in flexibility that enables the purchaser to buy one, two or all three floors, and to knock spaces together later if required. Interior arrangements can be previewed on a specially-designed computer program and buyers can participate in the design of their own façades and choose window types. The design permits mixed uses such as home offices or light commercial activities on the ground floor.

I visited several of these projects, and found little to separate them visibly from other suburban developments. While I admire the conscientious research that has gone into affordability, environmental impact and sustainability, the design makes little appeal to the noble potential of architecture to save us from the relentless sprawl of pastiche.

ADDRESS for locations of projects and further information contact the Affordable Homes Program, School of Architecture, McGill University, 815, rue Sherbrooke Ouest, Montréal, Québec H3A 2K6
INTERNET www.mcgill.ca/homes SIZE 225 square metres
COST $50,000 per unit, including land, at $350–$400 per square metre depending on choice of materials and finishes
ACCESS to some model homes

ACCUEIL
Réception
La Maison Redécouverte[MC]
Maisons de ville
The Next Home™
McGill University School of Architecture
Town houses
(514) 340-9770
Occupation juillet /July 1997
Une adresse de prestige à partir de 159 900$.

Downtown

Place Bonaventure pavilions

There is much affection among the design community for the original 1967 building by Affleck, Desbarats, Dimakopoulos, Lebensold and Sise. Inspired by Sant'Elia's project for Milan Station 2000, the Place Bonaventure is the most brutal exterior in Montréal, yet the Hilton Hotel on the uppermost floors is a vastly popular Shangri-la. In an effort to create a more user-friendly image at street level, a series of sheltering pavilions has been added to each of the many entrances (excluding, unfortunately, the hotel's). The design is based on a translucent sandwich whose thin upper layer is simple horizontal glazing, tilted slightly upwards towards the leading edge as a gesture of welcome, and channelling water run-off to the rear. The thicker lower layer is slightly smaller in area and contains a lighting system which attracts attention and offers security by night.

Despite the heaviness of the steel, there is something of the Japanese shoji screen about the panels, which edit out certain climatic elements while harbouring light within their surface. The structures, in a deep and warming burgundy colour, have a microsite-specificity that acknowledges ambient conditions of light, wind or general street conditions, either topographical or acoustic. They are fixed to the building by a variety of fastenings, sometimes relying upon it for support, sometimes leaning delicately against it. Further assorted steelwork acts in concert with the terraced landscaping to ease the transition between the concrete pavement, the concrete boxes of greenery and the concrete façade.

ADDRESS block surrounded by rue de la Gauchetière,rue St-Antoine, rue University and rue Mansfield
CLIENT Place Bonaventure Inc.
COST $2 million
GETTING THERE Métro line 2 to Bonaventure ACCESS open

Le Groupe Arcop 1997

Le Groupe Arcop 1997

Place Hydro-Québec

Ricardo Castro (architectural theoretician) It's a terrific city despite the fact that there are more and more holes. People come and they say, 'Was there a war here? Was Montréal bombed?' You start looking and you see the destruction that has been going on, how many buildings have been torn down to make parking lots.

It's all too easy to be pedantic about projects like this. The intention seems noble enough; it may not be very interesting or very beautiful, but it does try to do something with those empty holes. This particular one, adjacent to the newly refurbished Théâtre du Nouveau Monde, capitalises on the proximity of local thespian activity. The press release describes the project as 'an interactive cultural place for performances, exhibitions, projections, and information kiosks'. To that end, things have been left relatively flexible: it's flat, geometrically simplified, and the trees can be shifted about. It brings to mind French formal gardens where orange trees in planters migrate in- and outdoors with the seasons. Strong doses of colour in the alternating squares of green and red gravel blur slightly as the crowds disperse. Concessions made to performers include the free supply of electricity, and if you look closely there are little fixings in the concrete for canopies or tents. Given the strong tradition for street performance in this city I can't see this sort of formalisation being a great success with the artists, but the advertising dollars will have been well spent.

ADDRESS rue Ste-Catherine and rue Clark
CLIENT Hydro Québec
SIZE 2300 square metres COST $335,000
GETTING THERE Métro line 1 to Place-des-Arts
ACCESS open

Arbour, Berthlaume & Beauregard 1997

Arbour, Berthlaume & Beauregard 1997

Théâtre du Nouveau Monde

Dan Hanganu Actors are funny people. Sometimes it seems that they never come down from the stage. We expected to be on the same side of the barricade, but it was not to be.

SW Do you think it was a misunderstanding of the architectural language in general, thinking they could transfer one artistic language into another?

Hanganu There are many reasons. I find that actors – I'm talking about the directors here – have a very subjective and limited perception of the architectural language in particular. It may be because they always repeat things. Their creation is a quotation. There were a lot of misunderstandings and unfortunately the result is a regrettable compromise, and I'm far from being proud of it.

Having survived a checkered history of geographical dispersal and regrouping, the TNM is now all housed in one complex. There were three primary tasks to the expansion: the existing theatre was renovated and technologically upgraded; a new, much larger flytower was added and provided with a loading area with double-access from rue St-Urbain; a reception wing was added to house the theatre's administration offices, a rehearsal room, dressing rooms, and a foyer which in turn includes a café and a mezzanine restaurant designed by Luc Laporte.

ADDRESS 84, rue Ste-Catherine Ouest
CLIENT Théâtre du Nouveau Monde
STRUCTURAL ENGINEER Nicolet Chartrand Knoll Ltée
SIZE 5,000 square metres COST $12.7 million
GETTING THERE Métro line 1 to Place-des-Arts
ACCESS open

Dan S Hanganu, Architecte 1997

Dan S Hanganu, Architecte 1997

Ville Souterraine

The birth of the underground city followed on the heels of I M Pei's Place Ville-Marie in 1962, the first significant skyscraper to appear downtown. The property had originally belonged to the Canadian National Railway and included excavations dating back to the 1918 construction of a tunnel under Mont-Royal. Seeing the possibilities of a complex with as much commercial surface below grade as above, the developers installed a shopping precinct, two levels of parking and a marshalling yard, accessible via sunken wells in a vast, open forecourt. When the windsept 'place' failed to gain popularity with local office workers and shoppers, the access wells were glazed in and the principle of the underground city was launched. Almost every subsequent downtown development has plugged into this vast labyrinth, which now totals some 30 kilometres of pedestrian passages. Many downtown workers experience little outside this artificial environment, slotting their cars into one of its 10,000 parking spaces or arriving at one of the termini to the suburban railway service. Most of the large office buildings have monumental atria, designed as much to impress visitors arriving from underground as those who stroll in from the boulevards.

Thanks to the commercial success of the underground city, the municipal authorities have been able to act as overseers without having to fund much of the construction work. Extraordinary structural antics have been performed in order to make contiguous spaces available, and Montréalers recall the disquieting image of the Cathédrale Christ Church perched on piles while trucks went about their business on the construction site below. Downtown department stores, aware of emerging competition in the suburbs, see the underground network as a means of catching the consumer dollar before it goes home in the evening. This means cinemas, restaurants, gyms, total shopping. With the private sector footing the bill,

Various 1960s–

Various 1960s–

most of the attention is focused on maximising the retail space. Over 2000 stores now occupy rented space, accounting for half of all commerce downtown. No urban planning is involved, simply the negotiation of neighbouring real estate interests. The result is a pristine but rather banal sequence of trademark atria or multi-level shopping malls, with only rare glimpses of the surface. There are four main areas: from the McGill University campus to Place Bonaventure, reaching out either side to the Cours Mont-Royal and the World Trade Centre; from the new UQAM science complex to the Palais des Congrès via the Place-des-Arts; from the old Montréal Forum on Atwater to Mies van der Rohe's Westmount Square; and the area surrounding Place Berri.

Métro stations come as relief from the repetition of franchise design, each one having been commissioned from a different architectural office. Nine stations can be accessed from the hermetically-sealed environment, with 154 entry points all set within the envelopes of the nearest building so as to avoid direct heat loss to the street. Together they furnish a catalogue of styles within which the initiated can identify the hand at work.

Up to now the underground network has produced little of architectural merit, but it is nevertheless an urban phenomenon that has been much copied and continues to grow. With university campuses, libraries and arts complexes all tied in, the underground can hardly be avoided and, generally speaking, the architecture still begins above ground.

SIZE approximately 30 kilometres
GETTING THERE Métro stations Atwater, Berri-UQAM, Bonaventure, Guy-Concordia, McGill, Place-d'Armes, Place-des-Arts, Peel, Square-Victoria
ACCESS varies between sectors, but generally follows shopping hours

Various 1960s–

Various 1960s–

UQAM science complex, phase 3

The new campus promises to be a rowdy neighbour for Place-des-Arts, partly due to the nature of student activities but mainly because the ship-shaped President Kennedy building is so strong and so bold that it might just blow the nearby architecture out of the water.

SW Where did you get this form from?

Mario Saia The city required a gesture, so we began with a curve that pulled back from the boulevard de Maisonneuve as an act of deference to the neighbouring church. The proposal then went through a series of evolutions, with the curve remaining our important gesture. When we saw that the building was to be contained within an effectively rectangular site, we simply allowed the curve to inscribe the rectangle and that gave us an elliptical plan.

SW Given the urban context, I would be tempted to describe the form as organic.

Saia We had seen the budget and we knew that the design had to be as simple as possible. The laboratories were all kept to one side and the organisation is strictly rational. As far as the form is concerned, it is simply an ellipse, whose origins are geometric and not at all organic.

The brief was tight, demanding the use of traditional yellow brick as well as setting height limits to correspond with the surrounding buildings. It is interesting to note that the deferential gesture which was called for became the most controversial feature of the building. As they have done in many of their projects, the architects make references to unlikely sources, in this case the yellow brick and strip windows of the 1950s rather than the lines of greystone houses on Jeanne Mance and St-Urbain.

The campus will reform the urban block, with public spaces and path-

Saia et Barbarese, Architectes 1997

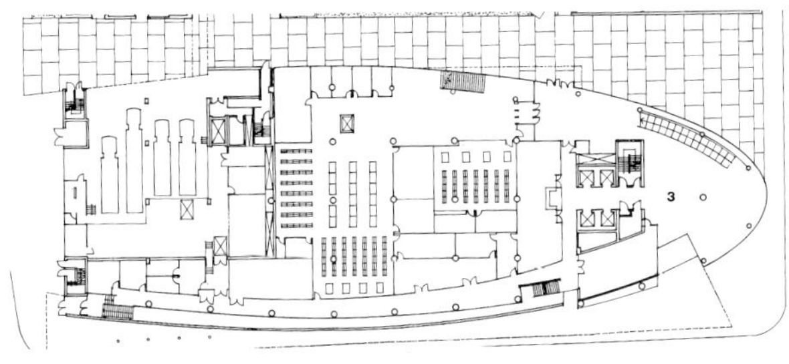

Saia et Barbarese, Architectes 1997

ways traversing the central area. A former foundry dating back to 1917 will be transformed into a cafeteria and occupies pole position in the ensemble. To the north, the Sherbrooke pavilion (the former technical school) is being renovated and furnished with a 500-seat auditorium designed by Perreault, Smith, Archimbald and Venne. To the west, the new Jeanne-Mance chemistry wing by can only be described as a safe design, and to the south lies the President Kennedy building. Still to be completed on the block are the department of biology, a theatre, a large multi-functional building, dormitories and offices.

SW With all the universities and schools being constructed at the moment, does this indicate that the government is making educational facilities a priority?

Saia In terms of building universities, construction is certainly over for the time being. The administrators had anticipated a steady increase in student enrollment – which is what initiated so many of the projects – but what in fact they later noticed was a gentle decline. These building projects have survived the decline in enrollment because the government sees them as a means of stimulating the economy – they keep the construction industry in motion and the workforce active.

ADDRESS block surrounded by rue Sherbrooke, rue St-Urbain, avenue du Président-Kennedy and rue Jeanne-Mance
CLIENT Université du Québec à Montréal/Direction Générale de l'Aménagement du Site des Arts IV (DGASA)
COST President Kennedy building: $43 million; Sherbrooke pavilion: $5.5 million; site integration $150,000
GETTING THERE Métro line 1 to Place-des-Arts ACCESS to lobby

Saia et Barbarese, Architectes 1997

Saia et Barbarese, Architectes 1997

Le VII-plex

Calling once more upon the generosity of the longest available dimension, Atelier Big City have stretched out the plan of a conventional three-storey triplex to cover the entire length of the site. This gave them a sympathetic proportion to work with at the street frontage and left a strip of landscaping – a leafy green space for the benefit of all seven apartments – to act as a buffer zone between neighbouring buildings. With this front-to-back orientation drawn up, the planning of the units fell into line. The services, bathrooms and assorted kitchen spaces are grouped together within a strip that hugs the southern dividing wall, jutting out at either end of the envelope to express itself externally and can be distinguished by its dressing of corrugated metal sheet. At the front façade this wedge-like projection shields the view of the houses further down the street. Central loft spaces are grouped around an entrance core which divides the building in half along its length. This releases the street façade for balconies that are big enough to qualify as terraces, and the extended procession to the front door gives an extra minute or so in which to see in or be seen.

Visible ageing hasn't tarnished the image of the luxury condominium. The blue-painted steel favoured by the architects is rusting through in places and the pathway undulates gently, as if ruptured by the monocotyledonous light fittings pushing up in search of the sun. When the empty site opposite is finally built on, the VII-plex will surely benefit; it is a building that reads very well up close.

ADDRESS 2120, rue Clark
CLIENT Émil Sadaka
SIZE 1000 square metres COST $600,000
GETTING THERE Métro line 1 to St-Laurent ACCESS none

Atelier Big City 1991

Atelier Big City 1991

Saint-Henri

Fortin/Shoiry house

Like the St-Ambroise project opposite, the Fortin/Shoiry house is a tidy modern bookend to a jumbled row of Montréal housing types. It also interprets the early modern style, this time to sculpt out a four-level single-family dwelling. Telegraph cables strung across both frontages pencil out freehand perspective lines and provide a subtle contextual layer from across the street, bringing out the harder edges of the design.

The attachment of the house to its neighbour on Rose-de-Lima rather than rue Proulx – the result of a bylaw stating that, effectively, whatever is orthogonally behind your front door is automatically your back door – givies the house an interesting aspect as it appears to 'face' the Lachine Canal while the front entrance traverses this façade laterally. A hanging metallic fire escape poaches space from the resulting yard and has become a framed pattern when viewed from within the house through a series of punched windows. Interior plans rotate around a centrally-placed stair whose open, steel treads and mesh panels to either side form a translucent element rather than an imposing block. The presence of young children has softened things up considerably.

As with many houses in Montréal, particularly those of the modern ilk, there is a surprising sogginess to the interior. This is the result of a timber frame nestled within the firmer exterior skin, so that no matter how rigid the building appears, you sense an unexpected physical give.

ADDRESS 70, rue Rose-de-Lima
CLIENTS André Fortin and Nancy Shoiry
SIZE 200 square metres
COST $143,000
GETTING THERE Métro lines 2 and 3 to Lionel-Groulx
ACCESS by appointment only

André Fortin and Nancy Shoiry 1992

André Fortin and Nancy Shoiry 1992

Georges-Vanier housing

This small development of ten units is a beacon of hope among some truly exasperating housing. The project has its origins in a pan-Canadian competition launched jointly by three housing organisations which called for affordable, inner-city housing for first-time buyers that would compete with the lure of the suburbs. De la Riva's prize-winning scheme initially resembled some of the modern projects of the 1930s, cased in glimmering white plaster and moulded into precise forms that spoke of the virtues of a pared-down existence. Denied his stucco, the architect turned to a concrete block that has quickly become the industry standard, blueish grey in colour and reminiscent of the local limestone.

The ten units are based on an original Montréal formula of an upper-level duplex with a single-storey apartment below for each frontage. There are thus five discernible houses, with the fifth split off and turned at right angles to form the corner. This is a brave move, demonstrating the possibilities for larger and more complex configurations. The principal façades are kept flush, with the upper apartments served by a straight stair that pierces through into a protected but exterior vestibule. To the rear there is the same formality of detailing except that the ground-floor apartments step out to form patios and partial roof terraces.

Plans for the upper duplexes are based on a rarely-seen lateral distribution, creating an efficient separation of spaces. However, the interiors are generally let down by poor construction and notable difficulties in coming to terms with new technologies such as the curved glulam beams to the roof. Where the window proportions become a scaling element to lend a touch of nobility to the façade, from the inside one feels a little cheated. There is a lack of internal solidity which may not appeal to those who are still to be persuaded that inner-city life can guarantee an adequate degree of privacy.

Richard de la Riva, Architecte 1993

Richard de la Riva, Architecte 1993

This is a design that is confident enough to invite thoughts of entire streets, adaptations for corner units and variations upon the theme. It not only takes an intelligent look at existing typologies but presents the city with an unusually tasteful prototype for further development. De la Riva confessed to me that he got 90 per cent of what he wanted on the outside and '80, maybe 85 per cent' on the inside. The scheme has won numerous awards and received extensive press coverage, but for the time being it remains one of a kind. One hopes that the points scored by the maturity of its appearance have not been lost by the growing pains on the inside.

ADDRESS boulevard Georges-Vanier at avenue Lionel-Groulx
CLIENT Service de l'Habitation et du Développement Urbain, Ville de Montréal/Les Enterprises Jules Maltais Inc.
SIZE 5 ground-floor apartments at 82 square metres each; 5 'maisonnette' apartments at 102 square metres each
COST $860,000
GETTING THERE Métro line 2 to Georges-Vanier
ACCESS none

Richard de la Riva, Architecte 1993

Richard de la Riva, Architecte 1993

Little Burgundy Sports Centre

The principle is simply to keep the wet area on one side and the dry area on the other. The plan is a parallelogram, cut in half by a central corridor with entrances at both ends, inviting an occasionally feudal local neighbourhood in through two equally-treated façades for some communal recreation. Once that line of symmetry is drawn, the architecture starts to address the practical concerns of the spaces it has created. Oversized brick is the cladding of choice – a charcoal grey anthracite to one side and terracotta to the other. Mario Saia was impressed by an 18th-century bank opposite, and picked up on the warm and generous dimensioning of its brown stone.

The swimming pool maintains eye contact with the outside thanks to a slot of glazing that raises one's view gradually from a park to the antique shops along the rue Notre-Dame, following the grade. Set into the wall above the paddling pool two circular windows with cross-eyed mullions alleviate the mass of the corner and take a pause from the racing lines of the glazing below. Changing rooms are security-conscious with no hidden corners, and parents are encouraged to change with their children. The central corridor, from which both the gymnasium and swimming pool are in full view, is lit by a series of light cannons overhead that throw spotlights on whatever comes into their path. The gymnasium features a glass-block window which takes the western sun full on and glows an ethereal blue like stained glass.

ADDRESS corner of rue Notre-Dame and rue des Seigneurs
CLIENT Service de l'Approvisionnement et des Immeubles/Ville de Montréal
COST $6.7 million
GETTING THERE Métro line 2 to Georges-Vanier ACCESS open

Saia et Barbarese, Architectes 1997

Saia et Barbarese, Architectes 1997

Police Station no. 20

Marooned among some low-grade industrial sheds, the police station's new entrance shines forth like a glowing badge coming to the rescue down a dark alley. This is no coincidence. The requirement to combine two stations, numbers 20 and 24, in the same building was also the opportunity to overhaul the public image of the force. Picking up on the notion of the uniform as a communicative mask, the architects have dressed the building in such a way that the thought of entering becomes a welcome idea rather than an act of desperation. The existing prefabricated concrete has been partly covered by a veneer of deep blue aluminium with shiny trimmings, and perforated so that the activity inside is rendered visible – exposed, even.

Various means of pedestrian access dominate the rue William frontage; there is a wide, processional stair; a notched stair for quick getaways to the side, and a sweeping ramp in low-tech galvanised steel that carries you across the garden (yes, garden), over a garage door and past the picture window.

Inside, vertical metallic fins replace the ubiquitous bars and bullet-proof glass – a move which involved considerable talents for persuasion. Lighting is subdued, the plastering is Yves-Klein blue, and the floors are softened with linoleum. Should you get hauled in one night, you might well think they have mistakenly whisked you off to another nightclub.

ADDRESS 951, rue William
CLIENT Communauté Urbaine de Montréal
STRUCTURAL ENGINEER M Marcel Gendron, Ing. (CUM)
SIZE 350 square metres COST $760,000
GETTING THERE Métro line 2 to Bonaventure, then bus 107
ACCESS according to penal code

Saucier + Perrotte, Architectes 1997

Saucier + Perrotte, Architectes 1997

St-Ambroise housing

People constantly refer to this project but, surprisingingly, never for the same reasons, because the qualities of the project reveal themselves over a long period of time. I would have been content to describe merely what I saw – there is a lot more to these houses than meets the eye.

The site itself was made available through a scheme entitled l'Opération Habiter Montréal, under the direction of M. Pierre Fontaine, architect for the City of Montréal Housing Service. Since 1991, the city has been selling off its properties, the larger ones to commercial developers and the smaller ones to anyone interested, who usually happen to be architects. Prices for single plots run from around $10,000 to $15,000. In terms of design, a certain sense of continuity must be achieved with respect to the neighbouring buildings, and codes followed, but other than that anything goes.

In addition to acting as architects, Pearl and Poddubiuk chose to wear several hats: developers, construction managers, clients and tennants. This gave them a sense of control that is appreciable in the end product. Four housing units were built around a west-facing courtyard to form a cluster on the tip of the Rose-de-Lima terraces. A 60 per cent street frontage requirement presses the façade outwards to fill the envelope. The image is predominantly early modern and reveals an attitude to massing, detailing and volume that expresses the subdivision of space within. Windows of restless proportions indicate both the light requirements of the inhabitants and what they may or may not want to look on to. For example, a view of the majestic art deco Atwater market tower warrants a large studio window. All three surrounding streets are used for access; doors are set into a head-high shield of brick, acknowledging the vestigial blue-collar character of the inner-city neighbourhood. Standard details have been noticeably tweaked.

L'OEUF, Daniel Pearl and Mark Poddubiuk 1996

L'OEUF, Daniel Pearl and Mark Poddubiuk 1996

Then comes the political part. The word that stands out in conversation and printed matter is 'holistic'. Scarcely a single material has been specified without considering its environmental impact. What I took for a compositional element on the façade is in fact a solar panel. From paints to linoleum floors, from drywall to heating systems, it's all been researched and certified as environmentally correct by the architects. For a moment we can set aside the esoteric agenda behind the design of contemporary space and concentrate on the history of the materials that collaborate to make it.

ADDRESS 81, rue Rose-de-Lima
CLIENT Les Habitations St-Ambroise
SIZE four units totalling 730 square metres
COST $500,000
GETTING THERE Métro lines 1 and 2 to Lionel Groulx
ACCESS none

L'OEUF, Daniel Pearl and Mark Poddubiuk 1996

L'OEUF, Daniel Pearl and Mark Poddubiuk 1996

Westmount

Dawson College

The opening of the new de Maisonneuve wing marked the end of a laborious struggle to bring together on one central campus several college departments that had been spread over 14 different locations.

The project began with the acquisition of the Congregation of Notre Dame's Motherhouse by Dawson College in 1985. Phases 1 and 2 saw the renovation of Omer Marchand's simplified Beaux-Arts building, which also happens to be the first reinforced-concrete stucture in Canada. The site straddles the border between the municipalities of Westmount and Montréal, rendering it subject to some 50 – often conflicting – building codes. Stringent fire regulations meant the removal of a handsome entrance stair as well as much of the surrounding trim to the windows and 6.5 kilometres of oak baseboard. A calculated risk was taken by specifying gyproc walls throughout rather than the graffiti-proof alternatives suggested by educational professionals. Most of the central volumes have been maintained and both the historians and former inhabitants seem satisfied that due respect has been accorded. In all, some 40,000 square metres of refurbishments were undertaken.

Phases 3 and 4 involved the addition of 10,000 square metres of space, most of which is underground because the maximum building envelope established by the two municipalities did not allow for sufficient aboveground construction. The respectful yellow-brick pavilions that now make up the de Maisonneuve wing of the campus conceal a huge complex below grade. Upon entering, one feels as though the architecture has been turned upside-down. An inverted atrium falls away, with escalators leading down to locker areas in the wings. From there, lifts descend to a triple gymnasium with its attendant weights room and changing rooms, then continue down to the mechanical and electrical technology departments below. Somewhere in there, there is a dance studio.

Dimakopoulos/Wigglesworth Architects 1987–97

Dimakopoulos/Wigglesworth Architects 1987–97

One marvels at the need to construct a 20-metre-high slurry wall down to the bedrock in order to extend the building envelope for an educational facility, especially when there are rampant skyscrapers opposite. The architects have tried admirably to bring in natural light but it has been unable to penetrate further than one level beneath the surface. I am still unconvinced that such architecture can be kept free of claustrophobia.

Back on the surface, the departments of office technology and computer science enjoy the above-grade west pavilion, and the central and east pavilions establish the position of the main entrance as well as a link through to the Atwater Métro station. The architectural treatment refers loosely to Marchand's Motherhouse. It includes the occasional bay in the yellow brick, underlined by a tidy course of foundation stone; copper-clad dormers, and a fan-light for good measure – all the right moves to achieve the blend-in architecture that one has become accustomed to seeing in Westmount.

ADDRESS corner of boulevard de Maisonneuve and rue Atwater
CLIENT Dawson College
SIZE phases 1 and 2: 40,000 square metres; phase 3: 8000 square metres; phase 4: 17,000 square metres
COST phases 1 and 2: $30 million; phase 3: $10 million; phase 4: $18.5 million
STRUCTURAL ENGINEERS phases 1 and 2: Nicolet Chartrand Knoll Ltée; phases 3 and 4: Jean Saia, François Deslauriers Inc.
GETTING THERE Métro line 1 to Atwater
ACCESS open

Dimakopoulos/Wigglesworth Architects 1987–97

Dimakopoulos/Wigglesworth Architects 1987–97

Unitarian Church of Montréal

A fire in 1987 brought the original Unitarian Church on Sherbrooke to the ground, leaving the diocese in search of a new home for their Westmount congregation. It was originally hoped that, like the Maison des Coopérants project, this could be funded by a commercial scheme, but the idea proved unfeasible. A site was found on de Maisonneuve and following a selection process involving three firms, Wolff Shapiro Kuskowski prevailed and had that rare pleasure of seeing their original concept follow a relatively unadulterated path through to completion.

As with many recent ecclesiastical buildings, the design is wilful, loaded with the desire to create a palpable spirituality. There is a complex mingling of influences at work. The decision to salvage and insert artefacts from the embers of the old church adds a funny twist to the rhetoric surrounding conservation and restoration, for whereas most contemporary restoration projects rely on glimpses of modernity, here we have dismembered glimpses of the past. The requirement that the church also serve as an acoustically plausable recital hall gives the interior surfaces and the organisation of the plans a rationale that is not obvious if one reads simply 'church'. The budget was kept down at $1000 per square metre, and you can see where money was parted with willingly and not so willingly. There are many sidelines to this creation story.

ADDRESS 5035, boulevard de Maisonneuve Ouest
CLIENT Unitarian Church of Montréal
STRUCTURAL ENGINEERS Nicolet Chartrand Knoll Ltée
SIZE 1400 square metres
COST $1.5 million
GETTING THERE Métro line 2 to Vendome
ACCESS by appointment during normal office hours

ARCHITEM/Wolff Shapiro Kuskowski 1996

ARCHITEM/Wolff Shapiro Kuskowski 1996

Westmount Public Library

In 1995, to the grave disappointment of Montréal's inhabitants and architects alike, budgetary surpluses of nearly $20 million in the city's coffers were used to write off loan by-laws in order to make the city effectively debt-free. In terms of buildings, this meant that nothing new was to be tabled. The Westmount Public Library, housed in an ageing gem of Victoriana designed by Robert Findlay in 1899, was left to fund its plans for renovation and a new extension by other means.

The architect has tackled the difficulties of an emotional and historically sensitive public by grafting on a structure of remarkable object-simplicity. This is all centred on a new 'street' which begins at a discrete new entrance off Sherbrooke rather than from the previous entrance overlooking Westmount Park. The 'street' is a programmatic critical path providing access to the old library from the rear, a subsidiary pavilion from an interstitial space through which the street now runs, and the new additions at the back which include the stacks, a reading area and a children's facility on the lower-ground floor. The sudden transformation of many of the original brick details from exterior to interior is a useful way of acknowledging the preciousness of the old building and raising it to the status of a stored item, like the book collection itself. Where there is no existing wall on the opposite side, there is glazing. This is the ambiguity of enclosure that the architect has worked with, inducing a feeling of observing the old building from the outside while being inside. The effect is crystalline and avoids the threat of materials interfering with each other or technologies clashing. Looking out from the glazing to the courtyard, you see yet more glass, this time in the form of antique greenhouses washed in lime against the sun.

The dimensions of the 'street' have a way of anticipating the spatial events to come. Just as you start to feel pinched, a stair falls away to the

Peter Rose 1995

right and the slot that it makes in the slab becomes a divisional device separating the corridor from the reading room, moving you past the reception desk. One detail introduces the next. Steel flats bolted onto the concrete frame are used as a secondary structural element, performing the delicate tasks, supporting light fixtures, providing cautionary guidance on the stairs. The resolution of junctions with bolts rather than welds imbues the detailing with its own private logic.

An existing, rather monolithic extension had to be knocked down in order that this one could be built and in turn provide a workable solution to the ever-increasing demands for shelf space and public accessibility. The plan looks dangerously ambitious in its attempt to bring so much together, but in this case the actual experience of the building is the better measure of its success.

ADDRESS 4574, rue Sherbrooke Ouest
ASSOCIATE ARCHITECTS Tetreault, Parent, Languedoc
CLIENT City of Westmount
SIZE New extension 2500 square metres
COST $3 million
GETTING THERE Métro line 1 to Atwater, then bus 138
ACCESS open

Peter Rose 1995

Île-Sainte-Hélène

La Biosphère

The dome was originally the US pavilion (designed by Buckminster Fuller and Shoji Sadao) at Expo '67. In 1976 the acrylic skin caught fire and vapourised in 20 minutes. Having been deemed undemolishable, the dome was donated to the City of Montréal, who have recently turned it into an ecowatch centre focusing on the aquatic concerns of the St Lawrence waterway. There are very good tours to brief you on the history of the structure, but nothing can compete with the raw power of the space.

All that announces the entrance is a small missing section in the shell. Once over the threshold, wham, the space begins to whirl all around you. Rarely do you get so much impact from so little architectural effort. Convex flips over to concave, as if the structural lines suddenly reconfigure as you penetrate the dome. The reality of these structures – their simplicity, the frankness of the openings – can come as a surprise.

In making good the interior the architects have kept things simple. Three of the four original decks have been incorporated, their deep steel beams now exposed and recalling the superstructure of oil rigs. Glazing has a bluey-green tint in keeping with the aquatic theme. Cladding materials are light, and views to the exterior maximised, reflecting the museum's status as a pavilion of enquiry rather than a container of incarcerated knowledge.

ADDRESS 160, chemin Tour-de-l'Île
ASSOCIATE ARCHITECTS Desnoyers, Mercure & Associés
CLIENT Ville de Montréal and Environment Canada
SIZE 4000 square metres added COST $17.5 million
INTERNET http://www.wul.qc.doe.ca/biospher
GETTING THERE Métro line 4 to Île-Ste-Hélène, or by seasonal river shuttle ACCESS call 283 5000 for opening times

Blouin et Associés 1994

Blouin et Associés 1994

Casino de Montréal

It took only nine months to transform the former French pavilion for Expo '67 into an extravagant gaming palace. Starting with a ten-day in-house design competition which fused the three collaborating practices into a working design consortium, a series of critical decisions was made, each of which led to a casino design that had no precedent in North America. Eight levels – of which six are devoted to gaming, dining, dancing and banking – were inserted into the existing structure, steel into steel. A large sculptural void centres the plan and allows for vertical circulation. Transparent lifts shoot up and down, escalators maintain their steady climb, stairs float precariously in space, all acting in concert like the rising and falling of fortunes. On the ground floor there is a decorative pool upon whose glass surface you tread very lightly, littered though it is with coins tossed in for good karma.

The casino takes in some 8000 punters per day who are dispersed into a maze of 1200 slot machines and 65 blackjack tables, set back in rows and islands away from the central cylinder and against the exterior shell. Glazing was introduced – contrary to the usual rules of casino design – and there are pleasant if rare glimpses of the Montréal skyline or the St Lawrence river. Carpeting is used to subdue the incessant drone of the machines but occasionally there are hard surfaces inlaid with tiny golden shards like so many raffle tickets discarded after the draw.

ADDRESS 1, avenue du Casino
CLIENT Lotto-Québec
SIZE 39 725 square metres COST $73.8 million
GETTING THERE Métro line 4 to Île-Ste-Hélène and bus 167
ACCESS call 392 2746 for opening times

Jodoin Lamarre Pratte, Le Groupe Arcop, Provencher Roy 1993

Longueuil water treatment facilities

Mario Petrone is one of only a few local architects to have pursued a free and organic approach to making form, rejecting the accepted maxims and references that have dominated the past two decades of local design.

Petrone responded to a plea from the City of Longueuil's administrators for 'a new architectural language', and the excitement that he subsequently stirred up led to his designing some nine pumping stations along the south shore of the St Lawrence. The designs vary from liberal to conservative depending on the political temperature of the local municipality. Artistic freedom was not easily won. Petrone recounts: 'There were concerns about the budget and the concept. The engineers especially were reticent about seeing this feminine aspect appearing within their work. My sculptures are really just the tip of the iceberg. On the inside they're just shitty pumping stations.'

The two most well-known stations are on the boulevard St-Charles, with the first looking somewhat like a cluster of mussels peeping out from the sand. An assembly of metallic strips houses the ventilation shafts and is covered in translucent fibreglass, enabling the structures to glow in the dark. The second facility is a series of five elliptical funnels, arranged in a staggered manner rather like the band on a U2 album cover. With the vast Jacques-Cartier bridge looming overhead, one is reminded that urban infrastructure can rule from both above and below.

ADDRESS 1315 St-Charles Ouest and 901 St-Charles Est
CLIENT Ville de Longueuil
STRUCTURAL ENGINEERS Martineau, Vallée, Régimbald Inc.
COST $3.6 million and $12 million
GETTING THERE Métro line 4 to Longueuil
ACCESS to landscaped areas above grade

Petrone Architectes 1985–88

Petrone Architectes 1985–88

Ville-Marie East

La Cinémathèque Québécoise

In the Cinémathèque – a multi-functional facility dedicated to the moving image – Saucier + Perrotte have combined the eternal seduction of the *camera obscura* metaphor with their love of theatricality. They have added an extension to an old school building to house a series of exhibition and viewing areas, including a lobby for public screenings, and research laboratories below grade. Administration takes place in the old school itself, which has been thoroughly refitted using a vocabulary entirely different from that of the existing façade.

SW Is there a metaphor for each of your buildings?

Gilles Saucier I wouldn't say so, no. In general we start by considering the components of a programme which are unusable from the point of view of establishing an overall image for the project, like the library or the offices. Once we see what is there, we apply the overview of the architect. Having done a few theatres in which we brought in a 'Dada' element in order to express our architectural vision, we now hunt for the genuine soul or essence of a project. In the case of the Design School this was the act of learning, the hands-on conditions of apprenticeship. In the Cinémathèque, the symbolic power of the *camera obscura* was such that it became the essence, not some forced metaphor where you see the building as one giant camera.

SW So it operates more subtly in this case?

Saucier Take the play on colour that we used. Everything is in black and white, apart from the projectors, which are contained in a wooden housing the colour of a 1910 camera, like the ones used by the Lumière brothers. The image that one sees within this universe of black and white becomes the reality, and the human space that one occupies is transformed into a fiction. The monochrome world exaggerates this

Saucier + Perrotte, Architectes 1997

condition by making the human seem even more colourful, *hyper*real, and therefore fictional. What the architecture does is to enable a confrontation of these two worlds through its apertures, and the metaphor is used as the means of establishing a more genuine sense of communication.

In fact the metaphor is legible in various ways although, sensibly, the architects have avoided being too literal. There are references to the structure of the camera and the various apparatus linked to it – used to particularly good effect in the entrance lobby. More pervasive and undoubtedly more powerful is the sense of navigating the architecture as if you were a piece of photosensitive film, constantly aware of the position and intensity of light, both natural and artificial. As you move, rhythms of light and darkness begin to alternate like the flickering of frames, conveying the sense of constructed time that is so crucial to the moving image.

A transparent lens-device clamped on the façade acts as a ceremonial link between new and old, placing the visitor within a container of images that are projected onto a translucent glass screen, creating an active special-effect of ghostly silhouettes that inhabit the image itself.

ADDRESS 355 de Maisonneuve Est
CLIENT La Cinémathèque Québécoise
STRUCTURAL ENGINEERS Le Groupe Teknika
SIZE 7500 square metres COST $ 8.15 million
GETTING THERE Métro lines 1, 2 and 4 to Berri-UQAM
ACCESS open to lobby, projection and exhibition areas; other areas by appointment only. Closed on Mondays. For details of opening times, exhibitions and projections call 842-9763

Saucier + Perrotte, Architectes 1997

La CinéRobothèque

The National Film Board of Canada's Distribution and Consultation Centre has developed a new form of urban oasis for an image-addicted generation. For those who question whether cinema has replaced architecture as the primary medium for spatial narrative, this facility brings the two together. But the excitement lies not on the exterior of the building but inside, where the shell has beeen furnished with the latest cinematic accessories. There is an electronic reference centre, a 142-seat cinema, a 20-seat videotheatre, and the CinéRobothèque itself, where the star attraction is a robot, headhunted from the spray-painting line of a Swedish automobile factory. With its spray nozzle replaced by two sophisticated hands (each with three fibre-optically equipped fingers), the robot now hunts and retrieves films on laser disc from 2340 drawers arranged in a horseshoe configuration. All this takes place behind a glass wall, calling to mind techno and DJs. In the adjacent viewing hall, where lighting and exterior noise have been carefully subdued by means of an intelligent system of blinds, there are 26 fibreglass viewing pods, equipped with computer screens and viewing monitors. Developed by the in-house technicians, these futuristic pods take into consideration every aspect of viewing (including various horizontal and vertical angles of vision), with the headrest fixing a viewing distance of 1.5 metres. They allow for individual viewing or viewing (non-contact) with a partner.

ADDRESS 1564, rue St-Denis
CLIENT ONF/National Film Board
SIZE 1430 square metres
COST $2.8 million including viewing stations and robot
INTERNET http:/www.onf.ca
GETTING THERE Métro lines 1, 2, and 4 to Berri-UQAM ACCESS open

Claude Gagnon 1996

Claude Gagnon 1996

Musée Juste pour Rire

This is a trippy experience which should meet the standards of even the most hard-core raver. Giant-sized vinyl records spin in the void. Suddenly you catch a glimpse of a woman about to plunge to her death from a chair that teeters on a balustrade overhead. Images are projected onto orbiting balloons which sport frilly tutus (the image is still and the screen is in motion, a clever reversal). A solitary loveseat lurks in the corner, 'reserved for Anita Ekberg and Marcello Mastroianni'. Whimsical furniture appears as you wander through the pervasive gloom, everything from Louis XV to 1950s to wrought-iron rococo. You pan from one exhibit to the next like Fellini's camera.

The architect's intervention is relatively simple. Taking advantage of the majestic industrial interior of a 1920s brewery, Laporte has employed a rigorous geometry of square-sectioned steel, all painted gold or silver, to furnish a square gallery that has become the centrepiece of the museum. An ingenious stair conducts you up the central volume towards a pyramidal lantern, the only remaining source of natural light. Also included in the project are floor-cushioned chill-out bars, a 180-seat cabaret theatre, a restaurant, shops and some office space. Not to be missed is the obligatory 1 per cent work of art by Marie-France Brière – several coffin-shapes set into the concrete slab entitled 'Do not disturb, I'm decomposing'. It may not make you laugh, but it's groovy enough to get a smile.

ADDRESS 2111, boulevard St-Laurent
CLIENT L'Académie Internationale de l'Humour
COST $8.5 million
GETTING THERE Métro line 1 to St-Laurent
ACCESS open except for refurbished offices. Call 845 4000 for times

Luc Laporte 1993

Luc Laporte 1993

Écomusée du Fier Monde

The most visible of the new elements that have transformed this 1920s public swimming pool into a museum are the balustrades and stairs. The interior of the existing shell has been uniformly whitened to allow the new geometry of welded steel to read like an overlaid ink drawing of varying line thicknesses, with the lines serving to define three levels of exhibition space. Raised balconies either side pierce through the concrete ribs and connect at the rear of the main hall to allow through-circulation, and now offer an enlightening view of the semi-circular vault construction through the high port-hole windows. Beneath the gallery, a sequence of bays, rather like private chapels, houses an intriguing variety of temporary displays. Finally, the pool basin itself has been filled in with descending tiers, extending the temporary exhibition space down through the ground plane and ending in a video grotto at the deep end.

Joseph-Omer Marchand was responsible for the initial 1927 design, which bears a startling resemblance to the Buttes-aux-Cailles baths in Paris – but that is a debate for the historians. There is much here to marvel at, like the persistent natural lighting, the pioneering attitude towards in-situ concrete, the sturdy mosaic tiling which peeps through from between the sleek new finishes, and the length and depth markings of the pool that seem to regulate a new order of black steel lines.

ADDRESS 2020, rue Amherst
CLIENT Écomusée du Fier Monde
COST $600,000
GETTING THERE Métro line 2 to Sherbrooke; bus 125, 14
ACCESS open Wednesday 11:00–20.00; Thursday–Sunday 10:30–17.00

Felice Vaccaro, Architecte 1996

Felice Vaccaro, Architecte 1996

Jean-Claude Malépart Sports Centre

Having fulfilled a 15-year-old obligation to the residents of the Ste-Marie quarter, the combined community and sports centre has already become an essential social landmark – despite the modest treatment of the rue Ontario façade, as if the long awaited opening did not require a ceremonious flourish. What the building may lack in decoration has certainly been made up for in the intelligence of the overall composition, which in terms of both massing and rhythmic continuity is laudable.

The site offered a narrow but critical frontage onto rue Ontario, pinched on one side by a garage and open on the other to a side street, leaving a corridor which opens out towards the rear onto a vacant expanse. The sports hall was thus positioned well away from the main road, leaving the smaller proportions of the community rooms free to communicate with the traditional street frontage. Inside, the L-shaped plan gives rise to two internal halls which allow you to gaze somewhat narcissistically down the sleek lines of the façade outside. Exterior and interior finishes alike are spartan but thoughtful, anticipating movement by changes in texture.

The bestowal of such a gift to an area considered underprivileged in both economic and architectural terms seems to have been duly reciprocated through its unhesitant adoption by the local community.

ADDRESS 2633, rue Ontario Est
ASSOCIATE ARCHITECTS Rubin et Rotman Associés, Architectes
CLIENT Service de l'Approvisionnement et des Immeubles/Ville de Montréal
SIZE 4200 square metres COST $ 7.9 million
GETTING THERE Métro line 1 to Frontenac ACCESS open

Saia et Barbarese, Architectes 1995

Saia et Barbarese, Architectes 1995

Place Berri

The park, approximately square in plan, is flanked by the bus terminal to the north, the Berri-UQAM university buildings to the west, a panoply of Ste-Catherine shops to the south and some unremarkable modern high-rises to the east. The gentle slope from north to south has been exploited by dividing the site into three bands corresponding to the descending morphological strata: the terraced slopes of the city, the water issuing forth from the mountain, and the mineralised fabric of the Montréal plateau. Similarly, the horizontal surfaces to the south of the park contrast with the grassy slopes of Mont-Royal. Lining the open central area on all sides is a buffer zone of trees, shade and benches, with wood chips underfoot – a tactile line of defence against the circulating traffic. Densely-planted flowerbeds face Ste-Catherine and two rectangular cages enclose evergreens and also serve as outlets for the Métro station. For five months of the year the flat central zone is transformed into a grand skating rink.

Then into this microcosmic representation of Montréal parachutes architect/artist Melvin Charney with his abstract sculptures. Three stainless steel structures built up of tortured modernist façades bleed into concrete water courses which descend the grassy sward and disappear occasionally beneath tumuli peaked with black granite headstones. The effect – funereal, Stygian – is perfectly appropriate for the punk-gothic characters who spill out from the bus depot and have made this park their home, but does little to clarify the symbolic intentions of the park.

ADDRESS corner of rue Berri and boulevard de Maisonneuve Est
CLIENT Division Aménagement des Parcs Ville de Montréal
CONSULTING ARCHITECT/ARTIST Melvin Charney
GETTING THERE Métro lines 1, 2 and 4 to Berri-UQAM ACCESS open

Peter Jacobs 1992

Peter Jacobs 1992

St-Luc Medical Centre

The medical centre is the most intimately proportioned of the sober yellow-brick hospital buildings that line a speedy section of the boulevard René-Lévesque. It bears the distinctive horizontality of the 1950s. As part of the upgrading, the upper-level windows and main entrance have been reconfigured. The architecture has consequently slowed down.

The most effective tactic was to change the plan, creating a staggered recessing of the glazing on the ground floor, which now partially conceals an access ramp from the road and permits views of the curved maple reception area within, about which the interior circulation rotates. Anodised aluminium is the metal of choice, and there are 'period' materials like glass block to go with the bent-metal chairs in the waiting area.

Less successful are the modified individual apertures with window sills adjusted to suit the vertical human dimension and racy strips cut into more sedentary TS. (There may not have been enough compositional strength in the original façade to take a new compositional layer.) A jagged metal stair which projects into the street from a corner aperture in the stone coursing is interesting as a design object but is unsure whether it should be welcoming or not. Such cosmetic treatment can be heavy and obvious, like adolescent make-up.

ADDRESS 190, boulevard René-Lévesque
CLIENT Hôpital St-Luc
STRUCTURAL ENGINEER Jean-Marie Maccabée
SIZE 1850 square metres COST $1.7 million
GETTING THERE Métro line 2 to Champ-de-Mars
ACCESS to lobby

Réal Paul 1992

Réal Paul 1992

UQAM School of Design

The jury for the Prix d'Excellence en Architecture 1996, awarded by the Ordre des Architectes du Québec, commented as follows:

> In this building, which is at once complex and monumental, the jury appreciated the little surprises that are both interesting and lively. Without wishing to make this school into a model for reference, the jury recognised its didactic expression and the exemplary value of the architectural composition to the students. Such a plurality of spatial solutions, materials, fenestrations and decorative elements requires a skilful hand in order to preserve a sense of unity between the large and small scales of the building. Beyond the concept and intentions of the dialogue with respect to the city and the environment, the jury questioned the potential function in real terms of the internal courtyard and terrace. Finally, in light of the ceremonious additions to the structure, the jury asked itself to what point it is possible to go without falling into excess.

What appear to be mixed feelings about Hanganu's work are expressed in the reaction of the architectural establishment, and the general approbation that comes with winning a prize for excellence is offset by a commentary that comes close to damning the building with faint praise. The School of Design building shows a high degree of tectonic legibility and has a vocabulary so broad that it borders on superfluity. As the jury states, it is fortunate that this is so well managed because it serves to remind us of the difficulty of designing without appearing to show-off. The simplest messages are the clearest, when the building itself comments on the act of designing and explicitly invites us to examine the way in which we react to it.

Dan S Hanganu, Architecte 1995

Dan S Hanganu, Architecte 1995

A few examples. There are non-repetitive level changes as we ascend the central canyon, installing within us a memory of each floor and department with a distinguishable architectural detail, be it a curved concrete balustrade or a steel cage. Navigation is concentrated upon our acquired architectural memory. There is a repetition of elements, with vertical ductwork contained in the same tubular casings as the concrete columns themselves, and often truncated without touching the floor surface, forcing us to distinguish between structure and services and thus creating a hierarchy among equals. The memory of the process of manufacture is displayed in the silo-like concrete bay at ground level, where the corrugated formwork has been suggestively raised as if to take another course, only to be frozen as a cladding material. Hanganu also comments on the three-dimensionality of things. As you move past or look down on lighting fixtures, for example, it is clear that they have been designed to be seen from all angles.

What should certainly be applauded is the extension of the office wing towards Ste-Catherine, the result of a hard-fought battle that avoids the school becoming marooned in an inner-city backwater.

ADDRESS 1440, rue Sanguinet
CLIENT Université du Québec à Montréal
STRUCTURAL ENGINEER Saia, Deslauriers, Kadanoff, Engineers
SIZE 10,800 square metres
COST $14 million
GETTING THERE Métro lines 1, 2 and 4 to Berri-UQAM
ACCESS open

Dan S Hanganu, Architecte 1995

Dan S Hanganu, Architecte 1995

Usine C

Having chosen to eschew the downtown theatrical scene by moving into an old jam factory in a working class area, the performance troupe Carbone 14 found itself in need of more than a simple renovation. The task was, rather, how to lend a sophisticated air of drama to the old industrial shell and justify the choice of site. Even the decision to have a site at all threatened to institutionalise the image of an itinerant, dynamic troupe. It was necessary to demonstrate that permanence of location did not amount to artistic stagnancy. The architects retained, Saucier + Perrotte, had already proved that fitting out an existing building could provide kudos equal to that gained from constructing a new building.

The Raymond Jam factory is a simple concrete frame clad in red brick. Most of its upper floors were stripped bare and turned into administrative offices. The basement, ground and first floors have received most of the attention. Within a relatively mundane rectangular plan, the architects have managed to sleuth out an axial procession of impressive diversity, cutting holes here, making bridges there, thickening walls with coloured plaster and inserting a streamlined glazing system. Approaching from the rue Visitation, we first encounter a brick façade from which a stair projects overhead, encased in corten steel and warmly rusted in, an initial declaration of passion for the industrial aesthetic. The entrance leads straight onto a concrete gangway, whose forms remain proudly displayed as impressions upon the surface – a second declaration. From here we look down into the boiler room which has been thrown open to the light in order to serve as a sunken café. There follows a variety of gathering spaces which allow for the procedure of disrobing, waiting, conversing and even stepping back into the fresh air of an intimate courtyard.

The rest of the complex is taken up by the main performance space and an adjacent, smaller rehearsal space. Along with the factory, these

Saucier + Perrotte, Architectes 1995

three volumes make a U in plan, centring on the courtyard. Seen from the exterior, the new additions have a lightweight feel, and meet each other with flush, refined edges. Colours are beige, pigeon grey and sand, all merging well with the brick which suddenly starts to communicate the texture and scarification of its surface. This is the first building by Saucier + Perrotte to take on the complexities of interlocking exteriors with the same rigour as their interiors. The best, however, is reserved for the less obvious rue Panet façade. By masterfully overlapping the cladding surfaces and stepping the glazing alternately backwards and forwards, a thin façade has been made to read as a rich three-dimensional surface, amplifying the underlying tectonics to give the impression of a series of deep volumes compressed down to the thickness of a few centimetres. From the inside only vertical strips of light in the eastern wall of the black box performance area can be seen. This in itself is a state-of-the-art flexible volume for 450 seats, with a stage that drops out of sight, a seating system that moves automatically from one configuration to another, and lighting gantries that cling to the steel frame overhead. A vast brick wall – reconstituted, not original – marks the far end of the space, making one final proclamation of love for the vocabulary of industry.

ADDRESS 1345, rue Lalonde
CLIENT Carbone 14
STRUCTURAL ENGINEER Martoni-Cyr et Associés
ARTIST Richard Purdy (chimney sculpture entitled 'Deus ex machina')
SIZE 4745 square metres
COST $6.1 million (with equipment)
GETTING THERE Métro line 1 to Beaudry
ACCESS for performances or by appointment

Saucier + Perrotte, Architectes 1995

Hochelaga to Maisonneuve

De Rouen housing

> One of the characteristic pastimes of our retired citizens is to rejoice in the spectacle of the street, to see or to manifest their presence without necessarily being seen. [This] housing provides for them an intermediary space between the public and the private in the form of a loggia-balcony. Similarly, the lift well opens on to glazed landings which offer a variety of perspectives over the city centre.

This excerpt from the architects' statement seems perfectly adequate as a programmatic brief in its own right. The balcony-loggia is astutely differentiated from the bulk of the building, its intermediary role made explicit in the subtlest of tectonic terms. In a climate not always sympathic to open balconies, the principle of the loggia is applied so that 'balcony' is elevated to 'room', and territory is claimed for all-season use.

The statement also explains the building's formal references to its urban context: the cream and red brick, the roof heights, the industrial language and even the Johnson & Johnson headquarters opposite, a much earlier Saia project. It seems to be very important in Montréal to be able to explain oneself in these terms. But the remarkable thing about the work of this office, perhaps illustrated by the referral to their own Johnson & Johnson project, is that their buildings are strong enough to transcend any given context and become reference points in their own right.

ADDRESS 2120, boulevard Pie-IX
CLIENT Office Municipal d'Habitation de Montréal/Module Construction
COST $3.1 million
GETTING THERE Métro line 1 to Pie-IX
ACCESS none

Saia et Barbarese, Architectes 1993

Saia et Barbarese, Architectes 1993

Johnson & Johnson head office

It should be noted first of all that Johnson & Johnson are no longer resident here; their much-publicised renovation is now the home of Vidéotron Télécom. Since the latter's occupancy there have been various changes to the architecture, but I gather that no significant impact has been made upon the central spaces, around which this building was planned. I compared my own notes with those of Witold Ribczynski who wrote a penetrating criticism for *The Canadian Architect* (January 1989), and despite the different style of executive that goes along with the industry, the description still fits.

Prior to this project, not too many industrial buildings had been subjected to gentrification, fewer still by a company like Johnson & Johnson. Although this company had been unrelentingly modern in its choice of architects in the United States, in Montréal it chose post-modern, a suitably up-to-date statement for a fashion-conscious corporation, further supported by the choice of older buildings which could provide inspiration. Cayouette et Saia, a young practice at the time (and with the noteworthy presence of Gilles Saucier) seem in retrospect to have used the project as a testing ground for not only post-modernism but everything from Beaux Arts to British high-tech. The fact that the building fits together so well is testament to the architects' ability to take a style at will and, rather than attempt to better it, place it into a meaningful relationship with another.

Two loft buildings, one dating to 1912 and the other to 1926, have been converted to office space. These are connected to the rear by a large new building which contains, in successive layers as one moves away from the boulevard Pie-IX, a grand reception area, a cafeteria and a gymnasium. Passageways on four levels connect to the existing buildings on either side. The ensemble thus forms a horseshoe-shaped court, with two significant

Cayouette et Saia 1986

features added: a water-tower-inspired service silo at the junction with the north wing, and a gatehouse reminiscent of the 19th-century Parisian *hôtel* closing the court to the boulevard. Planning is based upon the conjunction of two principal axes, one north–south and the other east–west, which meet in the grand hall where the point is ceremoniously marked with a thin column. Each axis has its own particular spatial progressions, one moves through what appear to be conventional volumes but a preferential reading might be a procession through a series of screens, both load- and non-load-bearing. Some are selectively permeable to light, theatrical even, suggesting a hidden agenda behind the post-modern trappings.

ADDRESS 2155, boulevard Pie-IX
CLIENT Johnson & Johnson Inc.
ENGINEERS LGL Ltée
SIZE 10,684 square metres
COST $10 million
GETTING THERE Métro line 1 to Pie-IX, then bus 139 south
ACCESS none

Cayouette et Saia 1986

Tour de Montréal

There is an exhibition of dolls at the top of the newly-finished tower, featuring a vintage Barbie as the star attraction. There is a message here – when dramatic changes in scale are made, proportions can often become unmanageable.

In 1987 the announcement was made that the leaning tower over the Olympic Stadium had been completed. The engineering was complex and problematic because the original stadium built for the 1976 Olympic games had been plagued by structural problems. Fresh from his success with the Parc-des-Princes stadium in Paris, guest architect Roger Taillebert had imported his ideas on the use of hollow, precast-concrete ribs, which for the Montréal stadium he doubled in size. Into the mix were thrown some ideas on retractable roofs developed with Frei Otto and employed on a Paris swimming pool, much to the delight of the French public. These he multiplied in scale by 12. The first signs of danger in the new stadium came when a 55-ton concrete beam fell off. There was a press conference.

Roger Taillebert I didn't build it. All I did was draw the architectural models ... an architect doesn't do an engineer's work.

Needless to say, the engineering required for repairs was as impressive as the struture itself. The stadium has had to adapt to its own size. Halfway up the tower, concrete was abandoned for steel plate as the process of casting at a 45-degree angle proved too difficult. You can just about distinguish the transition point as you ride the funicular lift that scales the outside of the tower. The plates of steel are set at 760 millimetres apart, post-tensioned to the existing concrete and making for a smooth join, but the real excitement is in the ride itself, which has a trajectory

Roger Taillebert et al. 1976–87

Roger Taillebert et al. 1976–87

like a hot-air balloon take-off.

The floor of the lift tilts with the curve of the tower, tipping you gently back towards the retreating horizon. At the top there are three public levels: a viewing deck, a bar with mirrors and a carpet emblazoned with the stadium logo, and the doll exhibition. The suspended kevlar roof that has been the centre of a long controversy lies taut below. It is possible that it will be retracted only once more – when it is removed. A project unveiled in 1995 proposed to replace the beleaguered roof with a non-retractable version in steel, webbed with an elastomere membrane. This time the clients insisted on a low-risk strategy involving 'tried and tested materials and engineering', if there is such a thing. Funds are being sought.

For the time being, though, the tower remains, like Barbie, a seductive and anatomically-perverse toy.

ADDRESS rue Sherbrooke Est at Pie-IX
NEW PROPOSAL 1993–95 Blouin, Boutros, Dimakopoulos
STRUCTURAL ENGINEER Structuras
CLIENT Régie des Installations Olympiques
COST $54.7 million
GETTING THERE Métro line 1 to Pie-IX
ACCESS open during events and for organised tours

Roger Taillebert et al. 1976–87

Notre-Dame housing

In the process of upgrading the east–west traffic artery of the rue Notre-Dame, the Government of Québec was obliged to use its rights of compulsory purchase and shave off the tips of several terraced rows. The result was a fascinating sectional view of the traditional Montréal triplex – the common housing typology in this quarter – and its accumulation of rear extensions, but it wasn't pretty. Rather than merely applying pitch to the wound the architects have tried to re-grow the tissue.

The creation of an end-event for the terraced row has been achieved by staggering the final two new buildings so that the cavity between back-to-back rows is practically concealed. With low-income tennants in residence, it was important to create a sense of belonging, and this has been interpreted via a series of variations upon a local theme. In a triplex, each apartment has direct access to the street. This results in the elaborate metalwork seen clinging to its frontage. The south-facing aspect enables the architecture to turn the corner and extend the period of improvisation, with crenelated parapets and *trompe-l'oeil* employed to solve the change in scale. This can appear overdone when seen end-on, but it works in the direct context of the adjacent streets. Two shades of brick provide the primary skin, with patches set back 10 millimetres as if retaining the memory of a structure once removed. Other materials – stone, concrete and steel – add to the effect that the architects, given several tunes on which to improvise, have replied with the score of a concerto.

ADDRESS rue Notre-Dame Est between ave Desjardins and blvd Viau
CLIENT Office Municipal d'Habitation de Montréal
STRUCTURAL ENGINEER Carrier-Zimmerman
SIZE 72 apartments on 11 separate lots
GETTING THERE Métro line 1 to Pie-IX ACCESS none

Mercier, Boyer-Mercier 1997

Mercier, Boyer-Mercier 1997

The Tree House

This building devoted to 'the tree' is set in a 40-hectare arboretum in which some 7000 species of trees and shrubs have been planted or relocated – a living encyclopaedia. The Tree House is also a collection in its own right, expressing a broad variety of tree-metaphors through material, structural and representational devices.

There are dozens of different woods both on show and integral to the architecture, from rough-hewn spruce to multi-coloured pine veneers. In keeping with a heavy emphasis on the didactic potential of such a structure, the tactile, decorative and even olfactory properties of wood are made apparent as you meander through the permanent exhibition. A concentric series of displays suggests the sectional rings of a tree, perhaps even the slow accretion of time. Each ring eventually leads you to the double-height internal avenue, lined and supported with glulam trees. High above, light flickers in from the west through a clerestory window with mullions set at erratic angles to conjure up the shifting ambience of a forest canopy. This axis provides a discreet access to a modest exhibition hall, then leads you out onto a raised viewing deck from which the real-life trees can be admired. There is also a sunken bonsai garden encircled by 200-millimetre-thick concrete walls with wooden copings, an unlikely but powerful reversal of the programmatic hierarchy.

ADDRESS Jardin Botanique de Montréal, 4101 rue Sherbrooke Est
CLIENT City of Montréal for the Jardin Botanique de Montréal
STRUCTURAL ENGINEERS Calculatec Inc.
SIZE 905 square metres
COST $1.5 million
GETTING THERE Métro line to Pie-IX and Viau, then park shuttle
ACCESS open seven days a week from 9.00–17.00

Charlebois Malo Péloquin 1996

Charlebois Malo Péloquin 1996

Plateau Mont-Royal

2949–9035

The name is the business registration number for the shop. The shell is exposed concrete with a heavy granite aggregate. The shelves on the walls are thick sections of laminated white wood, sanded by hand so that the grain is brought up. On the shelves are leather belts, bags, and cotton clothes either folded crisply or hung from wooden hangers. To get to the high shelves you climb a ladder which runs along a track from the front of the shop to the back. You can sit down in chairs which are covered with untreated 38-millimetre duck canvas. There are also comfortable armchairs in shiny black leather, well-worn on the seats and arms. The desk at the front is made from a very thick slab of solid, unfinished maple, and is supported by 250-millimetre steel I-sections, mitred at the corners and welded together, then bolted to the floor.

The in-house design team, Frederic Mamarbachi, Steven Cook and Robert Karambizi, showed me their studio – a big warehouse on the boulevard St-Laurent, with white-painted walls and bathed in natural light. This is where they design and make things. People were cutting cloth patterns and standing around large, square tables; workmen were sawing up the thick wooden shelves. There were piles of materials like calico and cambric, hessian and canvas, and the smell of tanning and sweet sawdust was everywhere. Their philosophy is clear like mountain creekwater and fits like the best pair of Levis you ever had.

ADDRESS 3526, boulevard St-Laurent
CLIENT Rugby North America
SIZE 2000 square metres
COST $30,000
GETTING THERE Métro line 1 to St-Laurent
ACCESS open

Rugby North America 1996

Mirrors are kept to the centre, suspended from a lighting rig which runs the length of the main salon like a laid-out mast, its spreaders fixing the mirrors in a vertical series. Continuing the theme, delicate halogen lights are spaced out along the stays. This system has been attributed to Jean-Pierre Viau, designed for Eclectic when they were on the other side of the boulevard. To one side of the salon there is an indigo wall whose concealed doors open to flash views of lime-green private cubicles, a private space for each client. There are generous views to the outer world on two sides; wooden framing surrounds the view to a garden at the side, while a more conventional aluminium glazing system frames the view to the street.

All the elements of the design work together to give you a break from the narcissism of having so much attention paid to your head. The big windows mean that there is always something to watch outside. The central positioning of the mirrors and the restriction of their dimensions to portrait-sized rectangles means that you see only what you *need* to see of yourself, at least until the procedure is over. Blow driers hum in tune with the Latin music. You think of that scene in *Paris, Texas* with Nastassja Kinski and the mirror.

ADDRESS 5142, boulevard St-Laurent
CLIENT Eclectic Inc.
SIZE 180 square metres
COST $75,000
GETTING THERE Métro line 2 to Laurier
ACCESS open

Saucier + Perrotte, Architectes 1996

Saucier + Perrotte, Architectes 1996

Enoteca Quelli Della Notte

A heavily-padded cylindrical vestibule eases the transition from bustling Little Italy to this sumptuous restaurant with its thoroughly visceral interior. The extravagant spirit of new-world Italianism is animated by a considerate approach to kitsch complete with amphoras, fractured terracotta mosaics and blue-velvet bar stools shaped like hearts. Silver, gold and chrome are used unabashedly alongside one another.

The two-level layout is inspired by the Grand Rooms of the 1930s. A scupltural plaster ceiling eddies overhead in the sushi bar and a marble stair sweeps down to conduct you into the plush fumoir for a post-prandial cigar. If all of this seems a bit dizzying, then concentrate on the light fittings. The various zones and niches of the restaurant and lounge are defined by their own finely crafted lighting systems which are used in concert with inventive mirror installations to extract a further dimension from each space. Ranks of suspended lights are multiplied across the double-height entrance gallery to form a rationalised night sky. Wall-mounted glass cocoons are made to float, and haloes appear around your head as you drift from table to table. The doors to the downstairs toilets are perforated with innumerable shiny keyholes for those who indulge in voyeuristic pleasures while waiting their turn.

ADDRESS 6834, boulevard St-Laurent
CLIENT Enoteca Quelli Della Notte
SIZE 130 seats in the restaurant and 60 in the lounge
COST $1.2 million
GETTING THERE Métro line 5 to de Castelnau
ACCESS open daily 12.30–15.00, 17.30–1.00

Michael Joannidis 1995

Michael Joannidis 1995

Espace Go

This is a theatre whose details set out to engage you right from the word go. A gently oblique ground plane on this stretch of the boulevard St-Laurent sets up a delicate reading of the façade's tectonic elements via the presentation of exposed metal columns – more specifically, the articulation of their bases, and the formerly dull sequence of frontages has been resuscitated by the insertion of a bright and communicative façade with mixed messages of transparency and translucency. An extemporised chatter has been screened onto the glass walls of the foyer as if narrating a hushed conversation before the performance. Solid volumetric elements are softened by the use of stone clapboarding, a product developed by the architects themselves.

A similar tendency towards dematerialisation is applied to the traditional black-box theatre within. To maximise the flexibility of the seating system, the supporting columns are perforated and the holes, while temporarily redundant, become a pattern that lends weightlessness to the steel frame. Both sides of the 250-seat amphitheatre are lined with regularly-spaced double doors, allowing for additional seating configurations and extending the dimension of the usable space laterally. A second cluster of halls connects the complex through to the rue Clarke, incorporating the offices of the company-in-residence, Petit-à-Petit, as well as a rehearsal studio which is open to the eager gaze of the passer-by.

ADDRESS 4890, boulevard St-Laurent
CLIENT Théâtre Espace Go
STRUCTURAL ENGINEERS Les Consultants Gemec Inc.
SIZE 2,500 square metres COST $2.4 million
GETTING THERE Métro line 2 to Laurier
ACCESS for perfomances or by appointment

Blouin et Associés 1995

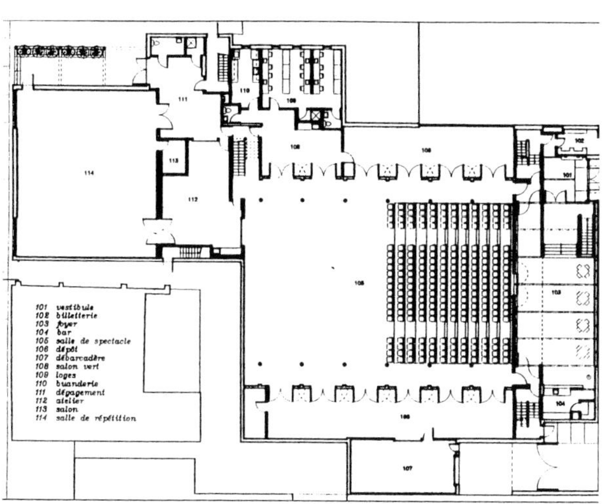

Blouin et Associés 1995

Grano

This restaurant/café benefits from the rare luxury of an unbroken volume that extends from the boulevard St-Laurent all the way back to rue St-Dominique, which in spatial terms translates into a heavy dose of linear trope. Most of the elements align themselves along this axis, like filings drawn to the flux patterns of a magnet. A standard aluminium-framed glazing wall has been 'drawn in' from the façade to act as a service counter and display. A raised seating platform hugs the wall opposite. Ductwork is cased in and suspended, running practically the full length of the restaurant. There is something musical about the way things stop, start and accompany one another, all heading in the same direction. Brash panels of colour pop out from the sides. At Grano the fare is all based on grain, with beers and breads replacing meat and potatoes. Suitably, chipboard and aluminium mullions have replaced rebar and bare brick as the next and lighter generation of industrial materials to be signed to the deco cause, with a retractable garage door opening on to the street, a detail that is now quite commonplace.

I looked in frequently, and the customers always seemed to be clustered at either end, avoiding the middle zone. Perhaps they prefer a view. Howard Davies, one of the architects, then told me that from the outside, most people see only occupied tables and think the restaurant is full. Forthcoming alterations will attempt to fill up the middle.

ADDRESS 3467, boulevard St-Laurent
CLIENT Restaurano Inc.
SIZE 300 square metres
COST $150,000
GETTING THERE Métro line 1 to St-Laurent, then bus 55 to Sherbrooke
ACCESS open

Atelier Big City 1996

Atelier Big City 1996

Maison Coloniale

The initial presence of this house is striking because one detects a sense of structural and programmatic risk-taking. Two towers, both square in plan, stand autonomously forward from a backdrop of interstitial space. This expresses the independence between the circulatory spaces and the bedrooms, living area and studios. The primary containers of the house are made to maintain a distance not only from their auxillary services but also from the urban fabric. Once activated by that sense of removal, all the smaller details and decisions become more deliberate, as if to confirm the act of separation.

The house has something of a work-in-progress feel to it. Signs of age are already setting in, and there appears to be no attempt to preserve it in its original pristine state. In its present state of flux, the house speaks of profound aesthetic dilemmas: the insistent imprint of nature upon the virgin surface, the fluctuation between disclosure and secrecy. The contrast between an assertive design and a casual attitude to construction evokes the complex relationship that exists between the use of the eye and the hand. The house is animated by a sense of informality: ivy has been taped to the walls with blue gaffer tape, the steel columns of the *piano nobile* bleed rust on to the leaf-imprinted concrete below. The project is an ongoing lesson in manufacture and consumption, like a building that contains the programme for its own destruction.

ADDRESS 4333, rue Coloniale
CLIENT Jacques Rousseau
CONSULTING ENGINEER Jean Touchette
SIZE 340 square metres
GETTING THERE Métro line 2 to Mont-Royal
ACCESS none, except for occasional exhibitions

Jacques Rousseau 1990

Jacques Rousseau 1990

La Maison de Poupée

Set back from a terraced row like the one depressed key on an old piano, this pied-à-terre is first brought to your attention by its non-presence. Adding to an overall sense of space opportunistically taken, the partition walls of the terraces on either side seem to suggest that they will close again one day, swallowing up the forecourt and re-establishing the urban solidarity. No demolition was involved in this displacement, however.

The house (only partially visible) is a former machine shop which was set back from the road for functional reasons. In the process of gentrification it was gutted, and one floor and a high-pitched roof added. The industrial touch was reapplied by installing parts of a corrugated granary which was imported from the Manitoba prairies and put to use both inside and out, first as a kitchen element and later as an offset gazebo which also serves to discourage visitors from becoming *too* interested. Such occupation of the forecourt contrasts with the capricious detailing and colour of the house and acts as a sober reminder of the public/private dichotomy of urban life.

ADDRESS 5253, rue Clark
CLIENT RDK Ltée
ENGINEERS Nicolet Chartrand Knoll Ltée
SIZE 180 square metres
GETTING THERE Métro Line 2 to Laurier
ACCESS none

Ronald Keenberg and Dominique McEwen 1991

Ronald Keenberg and Dominique McEwen 1991

Musée des Hospitalières

While far from being architecturally ambitious, the statement being made here is quiet but clear: this is a repository of relics, religious and medical. To house relics one should not build elaborate cases or buildings. To do this would be to interfere with the delicate rapport that exists between presence and anamnesis.

The new entrance is touched with modernity, but really amounts to a demonstration of high austerity. Inside, a 17th-century ceremonial stair faces the new functional stair, and with this contrast between the touchable present and the untouchable past established, the architecture sets you off on a journey that slowly separates you from real time.

The main exhibition is housed on two upper floors of an existing stone building, from which the new entrance inherits its features. The circulation is a loop per floor. Displays and partitions avoid all possibilities of becoming voluptuous. The attitude towards windows and external light is primarily that of the 'black box' and yet the interior surfaces are white, avoiding even the seductive qualities of darkness. Wood is not exposed but added, lending its sacred, rather than pragmatic, qualities to the displays. With so many objects wrestling with their own means of representation, the simplicity is a relief.

ADDRESS 201, avenue des Pins Ouest
CLIENT Les Hospitalières de l'Hôtel Dieu de Montréal
GETTING THERE Métro line 2 to Sherbrooke, bus 129 or 80
ACCESS mid-June to mid-October: Tuesday to Friday 10.00–17.00, Saturday and Sunday 13.00–17.00; mid-October to mid-June: Wednesday to Sunday 13.00–17.00

D'Anjou, Bernard et Mercier 1992

D'Anjou, Bernard et Mercier 1992

Orbite

The ground floor is reminiscent of a medieval fair, with a series of tent-like alcoves lined in velvet curtains suspended from candy-cane posts leaning out into the corridor. Caterpillar-shaped sofas cling to the walls, covered with a patchwork of recycled fabrics. On the floor there are over-sized linoleum tiles that recall those life-sized games of chess. The décor was a runaway success, so Viau was then invited to continue with the upper floor. This time he has opted for his much-loved scales and circles: there are circular coatracks lining the walls and an amazing number of circular, unframed mirrors. In one sequence alone I counted 50 mirrors, all of different sizes and inclinations, making a ratio of five mirrors per seat, though their combined effect makes it seem like many more. I asked the designer what was behind this obsession with circles and he replied, 'Grapes.'

Almost everything is suspended from the roof, including the hair-dryers, leaving the floor uncluttered. The mirrors do most of the work to divide up the space but there is also a large, scaly screen of translucent corrugated plastic and a curvy cosmetics counter in plywood that you have to wiggle your hips to negotiate. The colour scheme is predominantly pale pastels, recalling the golden era of Tupperware.

ADDRESS 1137, avenue Laurier Ouest
CLIENT Louis Hechter and Giovanni Bernardi
SIZE 220 square metres
COST $40,000
GETTING THERE Métro line 2 to Laurier, then bus 51 west
ACCESS open

Plateau Mont-Royal

Jean-Pierre Viau 1990

Petite Maison de Ville

The traditional housing model in this area is a split-level affair with access to the apartment above via an external, usually metallic, stair. It is these stairs with their high tolerance for invention that have become the signature image of the Plateau street, making standard terraced houses look as if they have grown beards and moustaches. Cassault and Deslisle took a radically different line by dividing their single empty site into two front-to-back strips. Each plan subsequently measures 3.8 metres wide, which is narrow but workable. The miracle here is how they have managed to make four levels out of zoning intended for only two.

At first there is nothing surprising about the interior proportions if you are accustomed to Montréal's long, skinny plans. The spaces are kept uncramped by highly efficient storage systems and sight lines are left open to remind you of the generous long dimension. The rear wall is liberated from the floor plate at the raised ground-floor level by a stair that descends laterally to the basement. This tiny cut-out has a profound impact upon your perception of the ceiling heights and is all the more pronounced by the egg-yolk-yellow colour with which the wall has been adorned. Up one level, the bedroom facing the street benefits from a void overhead where the roof begins its incline. A further flight of stairs leads to the studio into which sunlight eddies in from the adjoining roof terrace.

ADDRESS 5180, rue de Lanaudière
CLIENT Pierre Delisle and Lison Bédard
ENGINEERS Calculatec Inc.
SIZE 100 square metres
COST $75,000
GETTING THERE Métro line 2 to Laurier, bus 27
ACCESS none

Cassault, Delisle, Architectes 1992

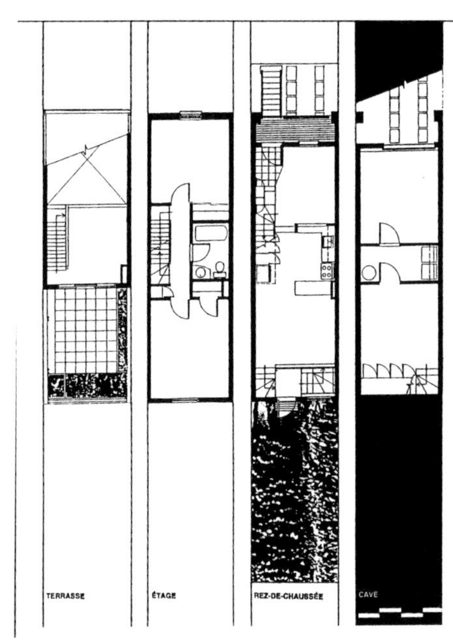

Plateau Mont-Royal

Cassault, Delisle, Architectes 1992

Pizzédélic

Jean-Pierre Viau is the only Canadian designer to have had his name used in an Absolut vodka advertisement. He is acknowledged as the man who brought the Canadian design scene out of the 1980s and into the 1950s. The Pizzédélic restaurant chain snapped him up and became the first franchise operation to commission a top-level designer, and the result is an ever-expanding network of funk across the province. Each new outlet is quite different from the last, and the colour schemes seem to get progressively wilder. It is a rare opportunity to watch the evolution of a designer at high speed.

In the St-Laurent branch (the first) the interior is relatively subdued. Viau concentrates here on one of his favourite spatial devices: scales. The walls are lined with overlapping plywood, narrow enough to allow light out from hidden fixtures, broad enough to recall the newspaper shelves of old. Variations in the stain, although all in natural browns and beiges, force any accidental references to succumb to the obvious desire to have fun. The kitchen area is separated from the dining area by more scales, this time in mottled glass and pointing downwards. The lapped boards of a wooden hull are brought to mind. None of this, thankfully, has anything to do with pizza. An oval bar is placed centrally so as to create a sense of diversity for the regulars, and is overhung by Viau's trademark motif, the circle, this time suggestive of bubbles which have risen up from the bar, spreading out at ceiling height with nowhere to go.

ADDRESS see Yellow Pages under Pizza
CLIENT Pizzédélic
SIZE usually between 250 and 300 square metres
COST about $350,000 per restaurant
ACCESS open

Jean-Pierre Viau 1990–97

Plaza Laurier

In an area abandonned by investors since the 1970s, the Office Municipal d'Habitation de Montréal decided in 1990 to rekindle some interest. The result is a significant consolidation of the urban fabric by way of 117 council flats, built in two phases on three independent sites.

Phase 1 expresses the strongest urban ideology. By acknowledging an unofficial right of way across the site to an existing playground, the architects have maintained an important link and thereby encouraged an extension of public activity that is customary to the street into the new project itself. This in turn has exposed the blank façade of an adjacent industrial shell which Boutros hopes will be snapped up and occupied.

Contained within an L-shaped floor plate, the building's sculptural modelling is arrived at by the convergence of two architectural typologies native to the area: the factory and the terraced house. The size of the block and its monumental features are inspired by the former, while the rhthym and scale of the articulated façade mirrors the proportions of the terraced row opposite. This combination of two quite disparate ingredients also gave the architects an opportunity to devise the internal programme. In all, there are 90 apartments on four floors. The lower two floors, which correspond to the 'terraced houses', are dealt with as such, with access both off the street and from a communal back garden. The upper two floors are for couples and have access from an entry hall made possible by the set-back for the right of way. It all connects together marvellously. By using a tactic already proven successful at their Cours-de-Charlevoix project, the architects were able to release more of the budget for use on the envelope by having the underground parking funded privately.

Phase 2 takes place on a more gentle, infill scale. On the Laurier site there are three new and 15 renovated apartments, occupying five formerly vacant 1930s buildings on avenue Laurier and one on Le Jeune. The

Les Architectes Boutros et Pratte 1994

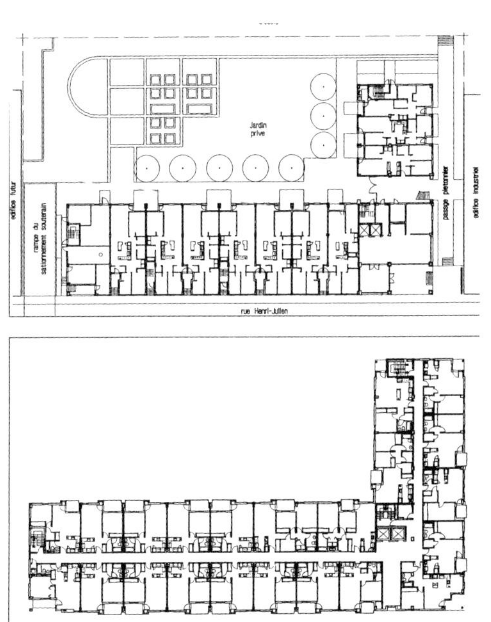

Les Architectes Boutros et Pratte 1994

Hôtel-de-Ville site comprises two twin buildings of six apartments each. While it is easy to catch the modernity in the new work, the natural fluency with which the vernacular has been read is also apparent.

SW I see such a powerful desire to use the existing vocabulary …
Raouf Boutros In Egypt we would build instinctively, we would not have to think about what would 'fit in'. In Montreal, though, we must tread lightly on history because we do not know it well enough yet to build instinctively.

ADDRESS 220, avenue Laurier; phases 2 and 3 are to be found opposite on the avenue Laurier and on the avenue de l'Hôtel-de-Ville to the right
CLIENT Office Municipal d'Habitation de Montréal
STRUCTURAL ENGINEERS Toutant, Ladoudeur et Associés
SIZE Henri-Julien: 7600 square metres; Laurier: 1230 square metres; Hôtel-de-Ville: 1120 square metres
COST phase 1: $3,567,000, phase 2: $1,035,000; total: $4,602,600
GETTING THERE Métro line 2 to Laurier, bus 27, 30, 55
ACCESS none

Les Architectes Boutros et Pratte 1994

Les Quartiers de l'Héritage

Presenting a clean and well-tailored profile towards rue Sherbrooke, this mixed-use apartment/office building was heralded by many as the solution for Montréal housing. In some ways the prediction was correct; there have been and will continue to be imitations of the delicate brick coursing and genteel geometry, as well as a collage-style incorporation of vernacular elements. The inclusion of offices and commercial street-frontage is becoming par for the course as new strategies are developed to revitalise the downtown core. What tends to go missing in recent versions of this type of housing is the astute use of section to create double-height, double-exposure apartments. This is a building which seems to be ordered horizontally – traditionally – when in fact the internal thinking is far cleverer, concealing a modern and inventive character behind a stiff and bourgeois façade.

The building consciously concentrates its mass along the primary artery of Sherbrooke, leaving a gap between itself and the neighbouring houses on Hutchison. This has enabled the architects to develop the dwelling type without being hindered by the complicated return of an L-shaped plan. It is interesting to compare the strategy used here with another housing project by L'Atelier Poirier, Dépatie at the Cours de Coubertin where a brownfield site has been developed with autonomous, parallel blocks, making for an open-ended and repeatable urbanism.

ADDRESS 377, rue Sherbrooke Ouest
CLIENT Sidcan Inc.
SIZE 28 units at approximately 110 square metres each
COST $19 million
GETTING THERE Métro line 1 to St-Laurent
ACCESS none

L'Atelier Poirier, Dépatie 1987

L'Atelier Poirier, Dépatie 1987

Le Théâtre d'Aujourd'hui

Entering the Théâtre d'Aujourd'hui from the street is rather like arriving backstage during a performance with the scenery shifted and waiting for a specific moment of entry. The whole architectural ensemble is dealt with as a series of solids and screens which interlock, interfere and overlap, and as a member of the public you gradually become a player.

From the foyer the auditorium is immediately perceived as an independent element, dressed in shiplapped steel plate in gun-metal blue, with the surrounding ceilings and walls appearing to retreat from it like the snow around a warm coal. The placement of such an object is logically integral with the evolution of the building itself, once a row of four greystone terraced houses into which a cinema showing pornographic films had been inserted, thus removing a large chunk of the original façade. The resulting void was therefore the primary intervention, and the next step was to place an object in behind it.

This done, the street-frontage is liberated for use as dressing rooms, administrative offices, ticketing offices and other functions which operate on a more conventional schedule. There is a large rehearsal room poised above the lobby itself, accessible via an enclosed stair with a dramatic, between-the-curtains verticality. A roof terrace offers views of the open night sky and glimpses of the street theatre that lurks behind rue St-Denis.

ADDRESS 3900, rue St-Denis
CLIENT Théâtre d'Aujourd'hui
SIZE theatre seats 275–300 people
COST $3.6 million
GETTING THERE Métro line 2 to Sherbrooke
ACCESS open during performances

Saucier + Perrotte, Architectes 1991

Saucier + Perrotte, Architectes 1991

Toqué!

The décor matches the spirit of the cuisine: flamboyant and lively. The fun begins when a rusted metal totem on the rue St-Denis draws your attention to an egg-yolk-yellow wall, perforated with irregular cut-outs, and then on to an unassuming front door. Upon entering you are conducted to a waiting area which, during busy periods, eases the awkward few minutes of idling by allowing you to observe the decorative antics from a thoughtfully central position. The plan divides a deep and dark volume into three intimate dining areas which are allowed to regard each other discreetly, either through a system of slots and nicks in the fragmented partitioning system or via rectangular holes framed in steel that have been inserted into a red-velvet wall, giving customers the delight of eavesdropping on *sotto voce* conversation. This is a restaurant where the artistry and attention are directed towards both the cuisine and the clientele, and so the emphasis has been placed on defining exclusive spaces.

From a purely decorative point of view, just about anything goes, from low-level crenellations of purple mosaic-like teeth in the front window to perforated metal screens which slide along to conceal the coat check. Like the best of nouvelle cuisine, the surprise of an unlikely combination is confidently supported by the sublety of competing tastes and the avoidance of unnecessary interference.

ADDRESS 3842, rue St-Denis
CLIENT Normand Laprise and Christine Lamarche
SIZE 300 square metres
COST $180,000
GETTING THERE Métro line 2 to Sherbrooke
ACCESS open evenings only, seven days a week

Tiiu Poldma and Raymond Girard 1993

Tiiu Poldma and Raymond Girard 1993

Hôpital de Réadaptation Villa Médica

Boutros and Pratte have robbed this bog-standard apartment block of its wallflower status. The building now serves as a rehabiliation centre, and in order to bring the new arrangement into line with existing codes, a lift was added and adjacent lobby areas created for each floor. This was done with great sleight of hand and an existing crevice in the plan was appropriated as the lift shaft with a new steel cage bolted directly on to the existing concrete frame.

The building communicates its revised architectural intentions through the use of three spatial extrusions. The first is that of the lift itself, pushing up and beyond an unremarkable roofline to create a powerful directional signal. In the second, the ground and first floor are brought forward and glazed in as one, hinting at a connection with the cornice heights of nearby houses. The third, an entrance canopy, strikes out along the perpendicular to occupy the ambivalent space fronting onto rue Sherbrooke. In all cases bright aluminium is used, making the new work distinct and authoritative. The architects were detemined to whittle their structure down and details are pushed to the limits of delicacy. The entrance canopy is a rare example in Montréal of architects challenging the over-engineering required for snow loads and wind shear. Inside, the angled first-floor balconies have been retained and in the cafeteria these can be seen refitted with glass balustrades, a luxurious touch for a building which would never otherwise hold such glamorous aspirations.

ADDRESS 225, rue Sherbrooke Est
CLIENT Hôpital de Réadaptation Villa Médica
COST $1.7 million
GETTING THERE Métro line 2 to Sherbrooke
ACCESS by appointment

Les Architectes Boutros et Pratte 1997

Les Architectes Boutros et Pratte 1997

Outremont to Côte-des-Neiges

Charles Bruneau Pediatric Cancer Centre

The new hospital wing for children suffering from cancer seems to emerge from the substance of the original 1957 building itself, clad in an identical yellow brick, with the junction all but concealed from view. The new addition can only be accessed via the main hospital although there is a street frontage which offers an interesting external view of the DNA-inspired stair, encased in its upturned cone of glazing.

Everything seems to hinge on this stair, which is appropriate considering the finesse with which it has been put together. Its adjoining landings on all five floors open directly on to the axis leading to the heart of the main hospital, while at right angles another corridor follows the line of the adjacent street. A curved corridor makes up the 90-degree arc between the two and services additional rooms. Unusual corners resulting from the radial geometry are used as nursing stations, common rooms and playrooms. Patient units, treatment rooms, offices and laboratories are all given positions at the periphery.

Playful details are to be found everywhere, from stellar configurations in the ceilings to a large stained-glass window that immediately alleviates the stale institutional feeling of the main hospital corridors. One senses that every hard-earned cent of donated money has been well spent.

ADDRESS 3175, chemin de la Côte-Ste-Catherine
CLIENT L'Hôpital St-Justine
SIZE 5000 square metres
COST $10 million
GETTING THERE Métro line 5 to Université de Montréal
ACCESS by appointment

Tétreault, Parent, Languedoc 1994

Tétreault, Parent, Languedoc 1994

Faculté de l'Aménagement, Université de Montréal

Seventy years ago Ernest Cormier, one of the seminal figures of Montréal's architectural culture, conceived of the university as an ever-expanding facility to be spearheaded by ambitious building projects. The new design complex continues to extend Cormier's vision and involves both the enlargement and reorganisation of the existing school with several departments now accommodated under one roof: architecture, design, and landscape, urban and industrial design. The original yellow-brick building was a convent, designed around a traditional H-shaped plan. Saucier + Perrotte have added three main elements – a studio wing, an amphitheatre and a circulatory system which ties together the rear extensions of the H to form an upper and a lower courtyard.

The boldness with which the design has been approached has resulted in a total transformation. Rather than adding a prosthetic limb, the architects have performed open-heart surgery. The heart in this case is a new amphitheatre in the central wing of the existing building, where all manner of structure – including concrete slabs – has been cut away to make room. Seating 400, it can be subdivided into two spaces seating 176 and 224, and its soft shape can be made out from the Côte-Ste-Catherine via a new glazed entrance.

SW Did you have to cut away all that concrete?

Gilles Saucier There was a chapel which had already been cut in two, so we decided to take everything out and focus on inserting one object that would demonstrate a new future for the space, defining its totality. So we anchored the ampitheatre there, large and rounded, and it became like an organ, a heart. It's glossy and shiny, a sort of dark-blood, liver colour on the inside and outside, and at the back it pushes

Saucier + Perrotte/Menkès Shooner Dagenais, Architectes 1997

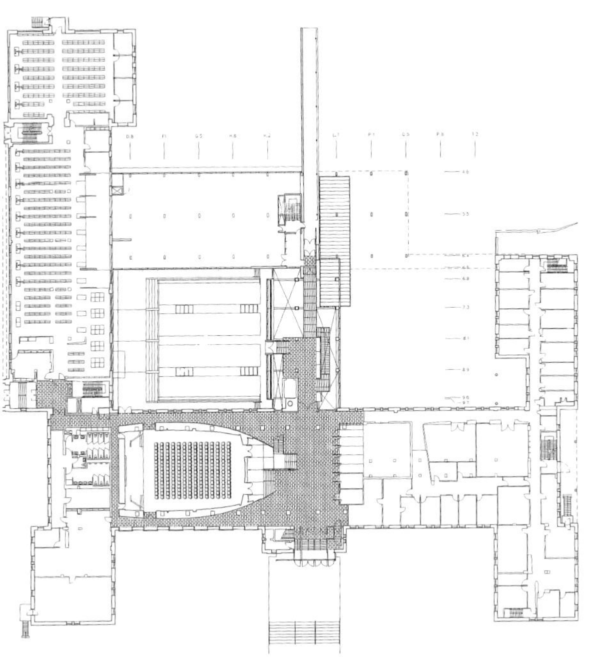

Saucier + Perrotte/Menkès Shooner Dagenais, Architectes 1997

> gently against the walls which retain it. The students' café is located around this principal space, and that's uncommon. Normally, public spaces like this are cramped up with heating and ductwork, but when you realise that the most important area of intellectual interchange is the café, you must reconsider those areas that are traditionally thought of as secondary – they could be the areas most conducive to creativity.

An axis driven through from front to back connects three separate entrances and links the amphitheatre with the courtyard and rear studio wing. At the upper levels it is flanked by the library to one side and the jury or crit rooms to the other. Natural light enters from the courtyard at ground level and via light wells from a hanging garden, enabling all 700 square metres of the four-storey space to be used for exhibitions.

The studio wing is a raised glass box, protected from the southern light by external aluminium louvres. Interior divisions are made using mobile screens so as not to interfere with the spatial continuity of each level. Ductwork and fluorescent lighting are impeccably ordered, leaving the exposed concrete ceiling free of clutter. An elevated corridor which closes off the central courtyard at the three studio levels features punched windows where you might wish to find them if you were an exhausted student taking a horizontal break in the corridor.

ADDRESS 5620, rue Darlington
CLIENT Université de Montréal
STRUCTURAL ENGINEER Nicolet Chartrand Knoll Ltée
SIZE 14,680 square metres COST $13. 14 million
GETTING THERE Métro Line 5 to Université de Montréal
ACCESS open to public areas at ground-floor level

Saucier + Perrotte/Menkès Shooner Dagenais, Architectes 1997

Saucier + Perrotte/Menkès Shooner Dagenais, Architectes 1997

École des Hautes Études Commerciales

The new business school (also known as the HEC) has 45,000 square metres of floor space. Upon leaving I was under the impression that I had visited several buildings, and it was the copious and fragmented nature of my notes that offered an insight into how the architecture deals with its incredible size. There are no easy generalisations – each façade contains its moments of blank tranquility, its ruptures, its opacity and transparency. There is sobriety, there is pomp and ceremony. The main entrance was inspired by the grain silos of the old port, and for once the scale is big enough to be credible. A plain rectangle with square, punched windows is held up by repeated cylinders that seem to merge into a singular mass. Buildings this big demand a narrative order that is equal to their size. The positioning of the footprint on the northern slope of Mont-Royal is the first communication to this effect, suggesting an ocean liner that has been beached rather than docked.

SW Of the people I've spoken to about your going against the contours of the land, some wanted you to be even bolder, while others thought it was a tragedy to set the form in that position in the first place.

Dan Hanganu It has quite a history, this project. I had no other choice.

SW You mean in terms of the building programme …?

Hanganu The school wanted a building that could be entered from Côte-Ste-Catherine and that would relate to the campus. A specific floor plate was required and there was no other choice. We designed a very straightforward building based on a 9-metre grid, inserted it into the forest where it meets the rock and made room for it! The gesture in the plan is based on Francis Bacon's saying, 'One can only order nature by obeying it.' We worked in a consortium with another office – not of our choosing – who had a different architectural culture. The team

Dan S Hanganu, Architecte 1996

Dan S Hanganu, Architecte 1996

was made up of some 50 people, so you can understand why it may have lacked oneness.

The programme for the building is set out in strata, with the upper-level corridors running longitudinally and giving onto intimate spaces which are deliberately distinct from one another. The classrooms, the library and the small lecture halls all have their own floors. Major public functions are grouped together on the ground floor and occupy monumental volumes. Communal spaces, large and small, all have a sense of theatricality which also serves to identify specific locations. There are catwalks, belvederes, flying stairs, cantilevered pulpits. Variations in overlaid floor plans use these devices in order to link, divide or interpret the volumetric sequences. Hanganu has an impressive arsenal of both materials and spatial solutions, avoiding the dangers of repetition. His winning idea, a curving curtain wall where the mountain has taken a bite out of the ground floor, is a big hit, probably because it symbolically acknowledges the concession to nature that the building was not allowed to make.

ADDRESS 3000, chemin de la Côte-Ste-Catherine
CLIENT École des Hautes Études Commerciales
ASSOCIATE ARCHITECTS Jodoin Lamarre Pratte et Associés, Architectes
STRUCTURAL ENGINEERS Lalonde, Valois, Lamarre, Valois & Associates (1991) Inc.
SIZE 45,000 square metres, 500 underground parking spaces
COST $101 million
GETTING THERE Métro line 5 to Université de Montréal
ACCESS open to most public areas on lower floors

Dan S Hanganu, Architecte 1996

Orange Julep

The enormous orange, a familiar sight to motorists who ply the Décarie autoroute, could be described as semiotic perfection. The present structure – a steel frame clad in large, dimpled fibreglass panels – dates back some 40 years. Its predecessor, built in the 1920s, had living quarters upstairs. The present incarnation uses most of its bulk as storage facilities, and the narrow slot at ground level doles out orange juice and hamburgers. Rollerblading waitresses zip back and forth, recalling the days when architecture of this sort wasn't haunted by the theories of Robert Venturi. Recent no, contemporary yes, and this is one of the most popular buildings in Montréal.

ADDRESS off autoroute Décarie at rue Jean-Talon
GETTING THERE Métro line 2 to Namur
ACCESS open

Ville de Mont-Royal to Villeroy

Jarry Park Tennis Centre

The new tennis centre sets about colonising a corner of Jarry Park, a flat and uninspiring plain scarred by mesh fencing and dotted with the occasional swimming pool. Being host to some major tournaments, the tennis centre cannot integrate fully with the open spaces of the park but signals instead a strong sense of occupation. Eight new indoor courts are housed in a modified industrial hangar, its northern façade lined with offices and services. The courts are overlooked by a café and pro-shop at ground level which peer out from underneath the offices, enjoying an intimate, panoramic slot that contrasts strongly with the emptiness of the court space. The architecture ventures beyond the mundane at the corners of the structure, where the entrances are dressed up to become cubic atria complete with ceremonial cornices, establishing a formal entrance to the service axis that runs through to a second entrance opposite the main stadium. A bridge at the upper level links the two structures. International tennis regulations dictate that courts follow a north–south alignment, and from the upper bleachers one senses the tangential plan of the complex as it creates difficult triangles against the rue Jarry. Four masonry towers anchor the structure at each corner, with a crescent gallery of press boxes making up the southern wing. The whole stadium sinks into monochrome except for day-glo orange padding on the air conditioners to the rear.

LOCATION southwestern corner of Jarry Park (entrance on rue Faillon)
CLIENT Tennis Canada
ASSOCIATE ARCHITECTS Provencher Roy et Associés, Architectes; Les Architectes Dupuis, Dubuc et Associés
COST $18.85 million
GETTING THERE Métro line 5 to Parc
ACCESS open for tournaments and major functions

Gauthier, Guité, Daoust, Architectes 1996

Gauthier, Guité, Daoust, Architectes 1996

Parc Métro Station

After it was bought by the City of Montréal in 1984, this imposing Italian Renaissance-styled building adorned with art deco Canadiana was renovated to accommodate a new Métro station.

The architects' brief was loaded with constraints. The above-ground entrance was to be installed in a rear annex whose final connection with the main building had yet to be decided. Both an existing sewer and a major electrical installation ran across the site and would have to traverse the platform areas below the surface while remaining accessible from above. In addition, a difference of 20 metres between the longitudinal axis of the old and the new stations ruled out a direct orthogonal connection between the entrance and the subterranean ticketing hall.

The architects have smoothed out the programmatic edges by concentrating on the sense of spatial procession which they feel distinguishes the Métro from other means of transport. At first you are made aware of the underground activity by way of a sunken garden into which a large periscope window is set, surrounded by ventilation grilles. As you descend the escalators, the wall surfaces change colour. The ticketing hall, a mezzanine overlooking the platforms, is spotlit by the triangular light periscope. The flow of passengers is echoed by curved, raw, in-situ concrete, both horizontal and vertical, with the larger beams recessed to take thin lines of fluorescent lighting and upstands punched out to give sneak previews of the tracks below.

ADDRESS rue Jean-Talon Ouest at Hutchison
CLIENT Bureau de Transport Métropolitain
STRUCTURAL ENGINEERS Saia, Deslauriers & Associés
COST $4.9 million
GETTING THERE Métro line 5 to Parc ACCESS open

Blouin et Associés 1986

Blouin et Associés 1986

Place du Soleil condominiums

The block of 12 apartments stands out from its surroundings in about as many ways as it is possible to do so – despite the municipal authority's insistence that it should blend in. So how did they get away with it?

The architect's statement begins '... the site is zoned semi-commercial, and will be the only building in this two-storey residential area to go up four storeys. The integration of this considerably larger building, without completely overwhelming the surrounding environment, is therefore the major concern of both the municipality of St-Laurent as well as the client', and conspicuously avoids mentioning the architects' motives. If you were to approach the rear or flanks of the building then you might nod your head at such a tactful response. 'Solution: a rectangular volume enveloped in red brick ...', the statement continues, sensitivity still holding sway, but then suddenly '... which is cut back where it faces the street corner in order to liberate a flight of scuptural imagination, playing with volumes, colours, shadow and light.'

What has been released is less fantasy and more a full-blown orgy of forms, with Meier climbing on top of le Corbusier and hardly a detail left untweaked. There is true joy in such unbounded excess, it leaps out from the leafy suburban context, letting us know that even the most prudent of municipal officials needs a little bit of this every once in a while.

ADDRESS 1545, rue Gohier
ASSOCIATE ARCHITECTS Lemay, Leclerc, Architectes
CLIENT La Corporation de Construction Tektopol
ENGINEER Les Consultants Gemec Inc.
GETTING THERE Métro line 2 to du College
ACCESS none

Diran G Loris 1992

Diran G Loris 1992

Ahuntsic to Cartierville

Cirque du Soleil headquarters

Everything that goes into the shows is produced here, from costumes to sets, even the choreography and rehearsal of acrobatics. With three shows running concurrently across the globe, this is the central thinktank of an extremely dynamic organisation. The architecture fittingly gleams with invention.

SW This is a very lightweight building. It seems to be made up of sheds – big, big sheds which are pushed towards each other so that the central space is interstitial – whereas in your other projects you talk about one fairly strict envelope and the definition of space inside that.

Dan Hanganu If you make that comparison, then several aspects must be taken into account. This is a circus, a bunch of serious jokers and clowns. The site was the old quarry – dump, really – so they behaved themselves very well by choosing this location. I did not have very much input in the programme, and they knew exactly what they wanted; a studio that big by that big by that long, next to that, and so on and so forth. I took all this and used the metaphor of the accident.

SW So 'accident' is the critical word?

Hanganu All their lives, those guys live in a world where the accident is a reality and a constant component of their performance. They laugh at death every minute. The basic *allée* [points at interstitial space on the plan] is for the ambulance, which was supposed to be able to get to every studio as quickly as possible. In the end this idea was abandonned but the great, central, linear space remained, bringing light into the building and facilitating a visual contact between performers and employees. So on the one hand, there is the basic intention to create a linear space, while on the other there is the nonchalant disposition of the functions accessible from it.

Dan S Hanganu, Architecte 1996

Dan S Hanganu, Architecte 1996

Accident (and its partner, humour) is everywhere, from the chainmail above the front entrance (part-curtain, part-hoisted-skirt) to the myriad bicycle reflector lights which adorn the rehearsal studio. The building is tremendously entertaining. Much is made of taking the industrial basics and creating a showpiece. Blue circus trucks add to the composition by plugging directly into the scenery workshops. In order to encourage interaction with the neighbourhood, landscaping is both pictorial and functional: it outlines a temporary big-top area, offers a grassy hillock as seating for an outdoor cinema (whose screen is incorporated in the façade of the main gymnasium) and even provides plantations of corn for the occasional outdoor roast.

ADDRESS 8400, 2e avenue
CLIENT Cirque du Soleil, Inc.
THEATRE DESIGN CONSULTANT Scéno Plus
STRUCTURAL ENGINEER Nicolet Chartrand Knoll Ltée
LANDSCAPING Schème Inc.; Architecture Aménagement
SIZE 15,000 square metres
COST $17 million
GETTING THERE Métro line 5 to St-Michel, then bus 67
ACCESS to landscaped areas only, otherwise by appointment

Dan S Hanganu, Architecte 1996

Dan S Hanganu, Architecte 1996

PetroCanada Fantasies

This is the first of what will become a series of projects aimed at blending PetroCanada's service stations into the urban fabric. The fact that PetroCanada came up with the idea comes as quite a surprise and might even signal a new, aesthetically correct attitude.

The architects have taken a fairly direct approach to the installation. Using the local code for cornice heights as a standard, they have reconstituted the building line with five aluminium cylinders. The effect is a little vague simply because the site – an exposed corner between two large traffic arteries – is more sub-urban than urban. From the parallax angles of the boulevard, however, the brashness of the pumping bays is pretty much out of sight. You pick up on the oil-refinery vocabulary of the structures rather than the signage or the station itself. With the primary task of screening achieved, there is further material for contemplation. A commentary on the construction process is taking place, with the cylinders appearing to be in various states of completion, even overcompletion. The ordering of assembly (or disassembly, depending on your direction of movement) becomes a narrative device. As a final act of goodwill, the structures are left open and lit, acting as shelters from the wind or a cozy nook in which to eat your hamburger.

Boutros and Pratte are working on their next intervention for PetroCanada, this time for a service station within the denser urban fabric at the corner of Mont-Royal and Parc.

ADDRESS corner of boulevard de l'Acadie and rue Sauvé
CLIENT PetroCanada
COST $200,000
GETTING THERE Métro line 2 to Sauvé, then bus 121
ACCESS open

Les Architectes Boutros et Pratte 1997

Les Architectes Boutros et Pratte 1997

Hôpital du Sacre-Coeur

The new wing has to deal with being grafted on to the back end of another, which it does by creating a gradual acceleration of external decoration that serves both to signal the main entrance and to take your mind off the services which are uncomfortably close at hand. The architects have mastered a kind of low-tech high-tech, with tension rods, bold cantilevers and superstructures in galvanised metal combining with wire mesh screens to form demi-volumes and alter your notions of the building's solidity. A high-level metal cornice acts as a brise-soleil and casts a textural shadow down the yellow-brick façade.

Proportions are picked up from the surrounding low-level blocks, corners finished in a similar fashion and the fenestration given sympathetic dimensions. All this reference to context seems fairly automatic, and reminiscent of the post-war functionalism that had such a calming effect after the raging expressionism of the 1920s and '30s. Where this building excercises its seductive potential is through that flamboyant entrance which invites you to examine all its intricacies up close.

ADDRESS 6555, boulevard Gouin Ouest
CLIENT Hôpital du Sacre-Coeur de Montréal
STRUCTURAL ENGINEER Jean Saia, François Deslauriers Inc.
COST $9 million
GETTING THERE Métro line 2 to Côte-Vertu, then bus 170 to boulevard Gouin
ACCESS to reception areas

Lemay et Associés 1997

Lemay et Associés 1997

St-Hubert housing

There is something of a medieval feel to this social housing project, and the secret probably lies in the scale and modulation of an internal path which presents you with alternating fronts and backs of apartments, as well as hollowed-out balconies and entrance stairs that poach space from the path itself. All this is indirectly thanks to a zoning law requiring the building to stay 4.7 metres from the pavement, a restriction which has pushed the programme into a welcome intimacy.

The site itself is a gentle slope that falls a total of 4.5 metres towards a railway track, flanked by the turbulent rear-ends of a terraced row to the west and a busy road to the east. Five four-storey blocks are nestled in and strung together along a communal garden path, offset along the axis and occasionally bridging over to make contact with one another. The apartments themselves give onto the interstitial spaces, underlining the confidence of the architecture to face itself. Colour provides an anthropomorphic system of legibility: brickwork is a uniform, pale mustard with pairings of crimson calling attention to the doors. Steel balcony rails are an in-between red oxide and window frames and copings trace out the edges in dark brown.

Some indication of the success of such a micro-community is the vigilance which it encourages among the residents. On three occasions I was stopped and asked who I was looking for.

ADDRESS 9656–704, rue St-Hubert
CLIENT Office Municipal d'Habitation de Montréal, Module de la Construction
COST $2.05 million
GETTING THERE Métro line 2 to Sauvé
ACCESS none

Mercier, Boyer-Mercier 1992

Ville Saint-Laurent and Dorval

Bois-de-Liesse chalet

Set in an inner-city woodland park, this rest-stop-cum-chalet avoids the cliché of the Canadian cabin by backing itself into the earth. The architecture that remains visible responds to this action by the articulation of its contact with the environment at large, its need to breath air and evacuate exhaust, the encouragement of circulation, and the desire to maintain a vigilance with respect to its surroundings.

Approaching from the submerged side, you climb what looks like an innocent grassy hillock in the otherwise flat terrain. Periscope-like outlet vents point at you from the other side of the summit, a ridge that is both created and barred by uniform bent-metal filigree running the length of a concrete retaining wall, sieving off whatever might drift up the mound. A curious entrance has been sandwiched between the roof fins which are bent over gently to acknowledge the prevailing westerly breeze. Beckoned down and into the subterranean shelter, you meet people who have entered by the more conventional route.

The concrete wall takes on an organisational role in the interior, separarating the troglodytic kitchen and toilet areas from the seating areas. The atmosphere is reminiscent of an alpine clubhouse, half buried in snow. Having camouflaged itself so well, the building is forced into a unique relationship with the landscape in order to announce its presence. As a result, it questions established notions of where buildings appear to begin and end.

ADDRESS 3555, rue Étingin, Ville St-Laurent
CLIENT Communauté Urbaine de Montréal (CUM)
COST $450,000
GETTING THERE Métro line 2 to Côte Vertu, then bus 213 south
ACCESS open from May to October. For information call 280-6678

Saia et Barbarese, Architectes 1992

Saia et Barbarese, Architectes 1992

La Chapelle de l'Amitié

A chapel of exquisite simplicity has been grafted on to the 1967 Unité d'Habitation of Swiss architect Max Richter, an avid follower of his fellow countryman Le Corbusier. Richter's strict apartment block serves as a home for the elderly, and its unfettered modernist spirit has been lifted further by the new addition.

Seen from the outside, the scupltural elements that combine to form the new chapel are clearly visible. To the eastern side of the main building, at its base, there is a vertical cylinder. This acts as a transitional form which connects the Unité to the main volume of the chapel which is roughly square in plan, surmounted by a roof that curves upwards from horizontal to about 30 degrees. Perpendicular to this movement a square 'wafer', acting as both roof and wall, descends back down, identifying itself as an independent element by a cladding of oversized slate tiles fixed with stainless steel bolts. Between this wafer and the main concrete volume there is a strip of glazing, top and bottom, left and right. On a clear, sunny day the consequences of this gesture are sublime. At approximately 13:30 the sun's rays separate the wafer from the rest of the volume, an effect that seems to transport it to the sky like a floating vessel and thereby supplanting the normal reliance on height for representations of heaven or other-worldliness. Into this floating element is inscribed the cross, giving the wafer a thickness, a reminder of its materiality. Further spiritual symbolism was to have been added by means of a canal to catch the water run-off from the inclined surface and bear it away to the nearby rivière des Prairies, but for the time being a car park performs this function.

The main entrance to the chapel is by way of the Unité's lobby. The cylindrical element is encountered first, nestled in a threshold area in which the tectonic elements are kept independent of one another by deli-

Lemay et Associés 1992

cate glazing. The material language is established: fair-faced concrete, stainless steel ornaments. Beyond the cylinder vestibule lies the chapel itself. After you enter the main building one floor up, your arrival within this simple space is immediately set into tension by the floating wafer which hovers above a ground plane that has since disappeared. Its detachment is even more obvious as you see the light entering from all possible points of contact. In an effort to maintain simplicity, the level of control has been stepped up: lighting is set directly into the formwork recesses of the concrete roof and the far wall is clad in maple-faced plywood, with only the fixing patterns giving the surface a relief.

The progression of direct light is at its most calculated here – a bright band that proceeds slowly along the knave and illuminates in turn the altar, the lectern, a madonna figure, Christ upon the cross and finally the tabernacle. At this moment the rest of the chapel is left in comparative darkness, and the inclined wall appears ready to depart, composed entirely of light.

ADDRESS 9165, boulevard Gouin Ouest
CLIENT Les Soeurs de Ste-Marcelline
FURNITURE Charles Daudelin, Louis Lemay
SIZE 800 square metres
COST $2.3 million
GETTING THERE Métro line 2 to Henri Bourassa, then bus 68
ACCESS by appointment

Lemay et Associés 1992

Dorval Airport

Dorval is undergoing rapid expansion and will soon become Montréal's major international airport, despite the considerable size advantage of Mirabel, L-J Papineau's vast inter-modal transport terminal opened in 1969. Deprived of some of its transport modes, the latter's Mies-inspired black box has never really been tested to its critical point or even filled to capacity. Dorval on the other hand has several critical advantages: it is close to downtown (which would normally be a disadvantage in the presence of strong lobby groups), it is well served by public transport, and it enables international travellers to connect directly to internal flights to other North American cities. Mirabel was just too far out on a limb. In 1992 the airport authorities unveiled their intentions to expand Dorval and the following year came the master plan.

The new Dorval International had to be designed with a semi-flexible layout in mind so that long-term plans could also be incorporated. The same went for the architectural language. Furthermore, the project had to be phased so that the normal operation of the airport would not be hindered while the construction was under way. Once the general concept had been established, the work was divided up among several architectural and engineering firms who followed the design concepts as drawn up by Cardinal Hardy et Associés. There were several clear tasks to be performed. The existing terminal was expanded by adding a glazed hall on either side, thus lengthening the concourse and maintaining the overall symmetry. The roofs have been constructed using double-bowed trusses whose aerodynamic section follows the design theme for the exterior work. A narrow, elevated street access to the terminal was widened, creating a more practical disembarkation area and generating interior space beneath. A wing-section weather canopy was added. On the ground floor, the resulting new entrances also feature the wing profile, this time

Cardinal Hardy et Associés et al. 1993–97

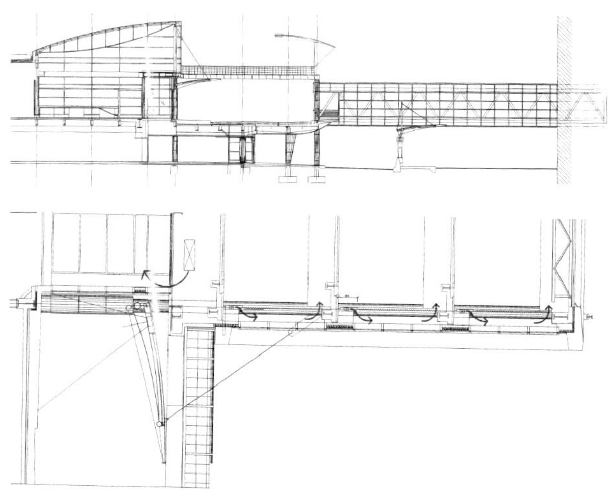

Cardinal Hardy et Associés et al. 1993–97

worked into the section as a taper to the ceiling which provides light for the loading and unloading of suitcases and people. The wing profile occurs twice more, in the curved streetlamps on the upper concourse and in a weather canopy at ground level that protects the central pedestrian aisle. Finally, with the parking garage that stands opposite the terminal a street condition is created, the two sides linked overhead by pedestrian passageways.

The adherence to and interpretation of a general design principle has led to certain incoherencies but the airport does feel up to date. With some work already begun before the general design strategy had been laid down, certain complicated adjustments had to be made in order to fit the new into the existing pieces. One wonders how far the theme can be stretched, and the question remains – can this airport avoid turning into another hotchpotch like Heathrow?

ADDRESS Dorval, Québec
CLIENT Aéroport de Montréal
MASTER PLAN/DESIGN CONCEPT Cardinal Hardy et Associés; Provencher Roy et Associés, Architectes
COST $150 million
EAST DEPARTURE HALL Régis Coté
WEST DEPARTURE HALL Le Groupe Arcop
COST $4.32 million
GROUND ARRIVALS Le Groupe Dessault Inc.
COST $ 2.97 million
GETTING THERE buses 172, 191, 195, 202, 203, 204, (209), 211
ACCESS open

Cardinal Hardy et Associés et al. 1993–97

Dorval Airport control tower

The tower is composed of three functional zones which are expressed in the material, volumetric and tectonic composition of the structure, like anatomical elements. The upper levels, roughly circular in plan, house a 60-square-metre control cab and its attendant service areas. A dark green tint to the 360-degree glazing coupled with a chiselled geometry lend to it the appearance of a finely-cut emerald set upon its point. The vertical shaft in corrugated concrete provides a vivid contrast of texture and sheer weight, and contains the umbilical functions of circulation, services and telecommunications systems. At the base there are offices, mechanical and electrical services and state-of-the-art electronic equipment rooms. The brief was technically complex and required the integration of numerous sophisticated systems. All design work was carried out using top-level CAD systems including in-depth ergonomic studies which helped in the streamlining of control operations.

The tower is a freestanding element in the airport complex, linked to the terminal building by an elevated walkway. Its construction was one of the first steps taken towards the upgrading of Dorval Airport and was kept clear of the design mandates set down in the master plan. The preliminary studies, design, working drawings and site supervision were all carried out by the same office, resulting in an apparently simple yet intriguing composition, somehow combining the aggressive directionality of the bunker with the transparency of a jewel.

ADDRESS Dorval International Airport
CLIENT Public Works Canada
SIZE 2,000 square metres COST $5.5 million
GETTING THERE buses 172, 191, 195, 202, 203, 204, (209), 211
ACCESS none

Fichten Soiferman, Architectes 1992

Fichten Soiferman, Architectes 1992

Île-des-Soeurs

Corot Row housing

The Île-des-Soeurs (Nuns' Island) has seen some of the largest housing projects in the city, and residents sometimes joke about the devolution of their island. Work worth seeing here includes a garden-city development by Cardinal and Hardy, cut short by a floundering economy, and blocks by Mies van der Rohe. There is even a petrol station by the great master. Hanganu's project was an early exercise in terraced housing.

SW I saw the Cremazie and rue Corot projects. Although very different, does one of them speak more loudly about housing than the other?

Dan Hanganu Cremazie is housing for the elderly, an eight-storey building. Rue Corot is just terraced housing. To my astonishment, Kenneth Frampton said it was the best terraced housing in North America – but there is a moment when I touch a definite type of confidence. There is some art deco in there, but it is the planning that is interesting. From every room you can see the river.

Frampton was definitely on to something. Rue Corot is a finely-tuned manifesto of urban generosity which appears to have been built only yesterday, save that the landscape has obligingly moved in. Its full set of tectonic gestures, from setbacks in plan to the articulation of the brick envelope, encourages curiosity about the inside from the outside and vice versa, drawing you into conversation with the architecture.

ADDRESS 265–99, rue Corot
CLIENT Delrive Inc.
STRUCTURAL ENGINEER James Teasell
SIZE 16 units, each 200 square metres COST $2.4 million
GETTING THERE bus 168 ACCESS none

Dan S Hanganu, Architecte 1983

Dan S Hanganu, Architecte 1983

Le Val de l'Anse

Despite being shoulder to shoulder with Mies van der Rohe, Hanganu's block comes across as impeccably tidy. The north façade is restrained, its prefabricated skin taut and teased up with scalpel-like precision to make room for the balconies. The concrete is tinted a pale, sandy colour for warmth. With secondary structural elements uniformly black, an anatomical hierarchy is legible, terminating with glass brick which reads as a translucent connective tissue. To get a sense of just how sheer this façade is, stand 50 metres away, clap your hands and listen to the crisp echo.

The block is rather like two towers joined invisibly at the hip, with two elevator cores on either side, each servicing two apartments per floor. The best views at the top are reserved for eight double-volume penthouse apartments. All 114 units are cross-ventilated and benefit from double orientation, northwards to the Montréal skyline and southwards to a lazy slab of the St Lawrence river. On this side Hanganu has given free reign to his tendencies to play with transparency and exposed structural elements. A row of ten three-storey townhouses has been extruded from the lower levels to act as a podium base, easing the transition from 14-storey concrete block to a groomed sward worthy of the best links.

ADDRESS 100 and 200, rue Hall
CLIENT Proment Inc.
STRUCTURAL ENGINEER James Teasell
LANDSCAPE ARCHITECT Jan Hoedeman and Associates Inc.
SIZE 128 condominiums
COST $17 million
GETTING THERE bus 168
ACCESS none

Dan S Hanganu, Architecte 1988

Dan S Hanganu, Architecte 1988

Eastern townships

Abbatial Church of St-Benoît-du-Lac

Situated in the breathtaking countryside of the Eastern Townships, this complex project has come to represent a catharsis in the relationship between the monks and their home. What was required of the architecture was far more than simply a new church. When Hanganu arrived, there was a project already in the making, with foundations laid and the floor-plans definitively established by the original architect, Dom Bellot. Equally emphatic was the desire that the liturgical requirements of monastic life not be interrupted by the rhythm of construction. Finally, there remained the necessity to translate the sacred language of building into modern terms, to restate the workable principles rather than borrow indiscriminately from other styles – to reassert the faith, in effect. Supplementary to this script was the frenetic detailing that already dominated the monastery and that had to be respected and subdued simultaneously.

It is well worth the 90-minute drive out to St-Benoît-du-Lac. It is also worth spending as much time there as possible, inside and out, watching the light and architecture combine to punctuate and often regulate the patterns of activity within. In order to experience some of the more delicate work that integrates the church with its adjacent buildings, the monks can, if given advance notice, conduct you to the private cloisters, belvederes and chapels. The church alone is a confident statement, reversing the role of the flying buttress by resolving forces within the envelope. One or two uncomfortable interruptions high up are all that detract from an otherwise clear spatial programme. Its plan is incorporated into a flush overall rectangle which also includes two towers and a cloister, proportioned so as to lend further authority to the existing tower which remains the largest of the three. The combination of volumes within volumes is expressed and disguised simultaneously by articulations of the building's granite skin, a technique which Hanganu uses to great dramatic

Dan S Hanganu, Architecte 1995

Dan S Hanganu, Architecte 1995

effect. There are hints of symbolism but rarely declarations. To the southwest there is a promontory which signals the intention to continue and complete the cloister by the addition of a symmetrical wing opposite the monks' cells.

SW There was something described to me by a monk as a mistake ... in the cloister. He said that the dimension of the lateral span was wrong, and that another face of brick had to be added to the columns, leaving a vertical gap of one centimetre.
Dan Hanganu It has been added, yes.
SW I mistook that detail as simply part of your own vocabulary.
Dan Hanganu The proportion of the space was too horizontal. I begged the monks to let me change it, and by doing that the joint makes it feel like a corner. Mistake? You could see it that way. I repaired something, but the intention was different, it had to do with the proportions.

It may seem unfair to include this snip of conversation, but it illustrates Hanganu's unrelenting approach to getting things right. The error is itself acknowledged in the process of construction, assimilated by its language, and the architecture enriched.

ADDRESS St-Benoît-du-Lac, near Austin, Eastern Townships
CLIENT Communauté de l'Ordre Bénédictin de St-Benoît
STRUCTURAL ENGINEER Shector Barbackie Shemie & Associates
SIZE 1700 square metres COST $7 million
GETTING THERE Highway 10 towards Sherbrooke; take exit 115 towards Magog and follow signs to Austin and St-Benoît-du-Lac
ACCESS to church, other areas by appointment only

Dan S Hanganu, Architecte 1995

Dan S Hanganu, Architecte 1995

Ste-Hyacinthe Professional School

As a result of the budgetary, programmatic and intellectual profile of professional schools of this sort, they have become a kind of architectural testing ground. Extremely large areas must be delivered, usually at industrial-shed prices, and social interaction ensured, meaning that any budgetary surplus should be spent on some real design, adapting the adage that you spend money on 'what you touch' to 'where you hang out'.

In this case the plan is simple and elegant; the formula may be there, but with some interesting variables thrown in. Four hundred students ebb and flow from the studio spaces into a common *préau* or indoor courtyard, intimate enough in width to encourage incidental encounters and long enough to allow for social avoidance tactics. The boulevard effect is achieved structurally via two rows of steel trees, grounded adaptations of an earlier plan to support the roof with cantilevered branches. The trees are a dry assembly of hollow steel tube, bolted together at the changes in section, which sets up a geometry that diffuses as it approaches the long barrel vault above.

There are nine different fields of study on offer at the college, all related to building, and therefore the interaction between metiers was prescribed as a positive contribution to the industry. In a sly allusion to the omnipresence of the architectural profession, the furniture and lighting was also designed by ABCP.

ADDRESS 1455, Casavent Est, Ville de Ste-Hyacinthe
CLIENT La Commission Scolaire Ste-Hyacinthe-Valmonts
SIZE 12,541 square metres COST $9.3 million
GETTING THERE Highway 20 towards Québec City; take exit 130 to Ste-Hyacinthe, turn left at McDonald's
ACCESS open

ABCP, Architectes 1994

ABCP, Architectes 1994

Théâtre de la Dame de Coeur

This gangly structure gives off wonderful sensations of a universe struggling for equilibrium. Performances take place after dark, when the giant puppets who inhabit the space take on a far more comfortable dialogue with gravity and the real world beyond the theatrical one seems less sure of itself. Twelve ghostly columns pull away at the roof rather than support it, accompanied by dark curtains which shift in the breeze like shadows. A white hose which threads through all 400 swivelling seats, circulating warm water, can be wrapped around the shoulders like a shawl when the evenings become cool.

Flexibility seems implicit in such an open-air context, but once again the designers provide sensation. The seating platform is raised 2 metres or so off the grade, allowing the stage to circumnavigate its audience. Balanced precariously on the edge, the platform exploits the level change for invisible backstage work yet remains perceptibly within the confines of the auditorium's spindly legs.

Several huts which serve the theatre are scattered about, trying to remain in the background. All that was called for in the brief was a roof, but given its success and the comparative clumsiness of its companions, one can only hope for more of the comic instability.

ADDRESS Upton, Québec
CLIENT CHAPEAU
STRUCTURAL ENGINEER Le Groupe Teknika
SIZE main roof: 1500 square metres; auxiliary structures: 200 square metres COST $600,000
GETTING THERE Highway 20 towards Québec City; take exit 147 and follow signs to Upton and subsequently the theatre
ACCESS open from the end of June until the end of August

Pierre Thibault 1995

Pierre Thibault 1995

Index